HOW TO GET THE MOST OUT OF THIS COURSE

SUGGESTIONS FOR GROUP LEADERS

We're deliberately not prescriptive, and different leaders prefer to work in slightly different ways, but here are a few tried and trusted ideas . . .

1. THE ROOM Encourage people to sit within the main circle, so that all feel equally involved.

2. HOSPITALITY Tea or coffee and biscuits on arrival and/or at the end of a meeting is always appreciated and encourages people to talk informally.

3. THE START If group members don't know one another well, some kind of 'icebreaker' might be helpful. For example, you might invite people to share something about themselves and/or their faith. Be careful to place a time limit on this exercise!

4. PREPARING THE GROUP Explain that there are no right or wrong answers, and that among friends it is fine to say things that you're not sure about – to express half-formed ideas. If individuals choose to say nothing, that's all right too.

5. THE MATERIAL It helps if each group member has their own personal copy of this course book. Encourage members to read each session *before* the meeting. There's no need to consider all the questions. A lively exchange of views is what matters, so be selective. The quotation boxes are there to stimulate discussion and – just like the opinions expressed by the audio participants – don't necessarily represent York Courses' views or beliefs.

6. PREPARATION It's not compulsory for group members to have a Bible, but you will need one. Ask in advance if you want anyone to lead prayers or read aloud, so that they can prepare.

7. TIMING Aim to start on time and stick fairly closely to your stated finishing time.

8. USING THE AUDIO/VIDEO The track markers on the audio/video (and shown on the transcript) will help you to find your way around the recorded material very easily. For each of the sessions, we recommend reading through the session in the course book before listening together to the corresponding session on the audio material/watching the video. Groups may like to choose a question to discuss straight after they have listened to/watched a relevant track on the audio/video – but there are no hard-and-fast rules. Do whatever works best for your group!

9. THE TRANSCRIPT is included at the end of the course book. It is a written record of the audio/video material and will be invaluable as you prepare. Group members will benefit from having their own copy.

RUNNING A VIRTUAL HOUSE GROUP AND SHARING AUDIO/VIDEO

To run your virtual group, use software such as Zoom or Google Meet, and use the 'Share Screen' function to share the audio/video with your group.

HOW TO DOWNLOAD THE AUDIO AND VIDEO

To access the downloadable videos that come with the course book, go to https://spckpublishing. co.uk/the-gift-of-christ-york-courses-video. You can watch and download the videos there. To download the audio, go to https://spckpublishing.co.uk/the-gift-of-christ-york-courses-audio and use the code TheGiftOfChristMP3 to purchase the audio for free on the site.

T0004225

The full list of available formats is as follows:

- Course book including transcript of video and access to video/audio downloads (paperback 978 1 91584 331 9)
- Course book including transcript of video and access to video/audio downloads (eBook 978 1 915843 33 3, ePub and Mobi files provided)
- Participants' book including transcript of video: pack of 5 (Paperback 978 1 915843 32 6)
- Participants' book including transcript of video (eBook 978 1 915843 34 0, both ePub and Mobi files provided)
- Video of discussion to support *The Gift of Christ*, available via the course book with access to audio and video downloads
- Audio book of discussion to support *The Gift of Christ* (audio/digital download 978 1 915843 35 7)
- Audio book of discussion to support *The Gift of Christ* (CD 978 1 915843 36 4)

THE GIFT OF CHRIST

Responding and living fruitfully

An ecumenical course in five sessions

Olivia Amartey

CONTENTS

Sessions

Transcript

SESSION 1
THE GENEROSITY OF GOD

A WOW MOMENT

I arrived on a cold, rainy day and was met by the hosts of the retreat centre I had booked. After being ushered inside, I was shown where I would be spending the week of my retreat and, as the door opened, my jaw dropped. The bedroom wasn't the small dorm room I had expected: rather, it was a huge 30-foot by 20-foot space into which my house could pretty much have fitted! Seeing the sheer delight etched on my face, one of my hosts said, 'Come with me – there's more!' She then walked me into the sitting room, beautifully furnished with several large, soft lounging sofas. It was even bigger than the bedroom, having its own dining room and adjoining kitchen. As I looked out through the huge expanse of glass framing the ocean, I was completely overwhelmed.

Why? You see, there was a backstory. The use of this space came by way of invitation and had been offered freely. I was the recipient of so much more than I had anticipated. For me, it was a WOW moment. I hadn't deserved what I received, but my hosts took such pleasure in unveiling this gift, and watching my facial expressions and reactions as I went from room to room. Their joy mirrored my own.

'You have not lived today until you have done something for someone who can never repay you.'
JOHN BUNYAN

'Joy is the infallible sign of the presence of God.'
PIERRE TEILHARD DE CHARDIN

Can you recall a moment when you have been overjoyed or overwhelmed by the generosity of others? Often when we think of generosity, we associate it with something of monetary value. For Western Christians, this is not an unusual response. Driven by our bias towards accumulation and materialism, we easily recognise when generosity is expressed in this way. Yet, when I reflect on the times that I have felt most overwhelmed, there's been no financial component at all. I think of a small act of love; a word of encouragement at a difficult time; a hand-delivered meal; an unexpected call or visit; a focused, listening ear. All these have been gratefully received because – insignificant and trivial as they may seem – they are living demonstrations of how perfectly God loves us and blesses us through the generosity of others.

God is a giver. As Christians, we instinctively know this. But let's take a contemplative 'selah' moment and pause to think seriously about the generosity of God. God not only gives, he also does so lavishly and abundantly. It is his very nature to give, and the Scriptures testify repeatedly about how we are the focus of God's love and recipients of his blessing. Grasping this truth liberates us to enjoy the security we're offered. It also helps us understand that God calls us to steward his extraordinary generosity so that out of the overflow of his love we become a source of blessing to others.

'Being generous of spirit is a wonderful way to live.'
PETE SEEGER

'Love is the desire for another's happiness.'
MARTY RUBIN

THE PERFECT GIFT

Just think how much easier your life would be if you had an innate ability to buy the perfect gift – one perfectly suited to the person for whom it was bought. Don't underestimate this skill, because I think it would be akin to a superpower! Christmases, birthdays, weddings and the pressures they produce would become a thing of the past. Your friends, colleagues and loved ones would consider themselves to be immensely blessed if they knew they were on *your* present list. No longer would they be the recipient of an ill-fitting sweater or a bland, generic gift voucher . . .

'Ugh. Would that Christmas could just *be*, without presents. It is just so stupid, everyone exhausting themselves, miserably haemorrhaging money on pointless items nobody wants: no longer tokens of love but angst-ridden solutions to problems.'
HELEN FIELDING, BRIDGET JONES'S DIARY

. . . Instead, they would receive a present that was uniquely matched to them, fitting their personality and accommodating their preferences. God has done just that. He has endowed us with a superpower! Through the gift of the Holy Spirit, he has empowered each one of us to become his perfect gift to one another.

When it comes to giving yourself away to others, you've probably felt inadequate. I know I have! Inadequacy, the fear of not being good enough, is one of the reasons why we may not consider ourselves to be recipients and bearers of God's gift to others. This debilitating fear is experienced by most people at one point or another. We naturally observe our acquaintances, colleagues and peers, assessing their skills, prowess and competencies, and conclude that other people are far more accomplished than we are. This feeling of inadequacy may be especially acute when we compare our seemingly small accomplishments with the awesome exploits of certain men and women in the Scriptures. We may (wrongly) conclude that, in God's eyes, we simply don't measure up and never will.

'I haven't any language weak enough to depict the weakness of my spiritual life. If I weakened it enough it would cease to be language at all. Like when you try to turn the gas-ring a little lower still, and it merely goes out.'
C. S. LEWIS

If we find ourselves at this point, we need to go back to God, the giver of all good things, and declare his truth: that we are 'heirs of God and co-heirs with Christ' (Romans 8:17). This is not wishful thinking; it is a fact! Because God has given us Christ, the greatest gift of all, we are now living, breathing, tangible reflections of his divine values, as he works in us and through our yielded lives.

Lent and Easter are 'selah' seasons within the calendar year that, if used wisely, will lead us to review, prune and strip away bushy foliage to reveal the taproots of our faith. These times of intentional reflection will help us to refocus and reorient ourselves towards God, and to realign our purposes with his.

Reading the Bible, we discover that God gives a special gift to each one of us. Our gift will not only reflect our particular personality through its use; it will also reflect God's image as the Giver of the gift. Gifts are part of his plan to work in the world, and because God gives them supernaturally, they are only accessed and activated through his enabling Holy Spirit. It is our responsibility to discover, steward and hone our gift to glorify him and reveal his kingdom.

Spiritual gifts are different from natural talents or abilities (such as an aptitude for music or sports), which are generationally and genetically inherited and nurtured in the context of one's family.

'When I stand before God at the end of my life, I would hope that I would not have a single bit of talent left, and could say, "I used everything you gave me."'
ERMA BOMBECK

However, as Warner Harris explains, 'Natural talents are just that: "natural" . . . [They] are imparted at our natural birth; spiritual gifts are given when we are born again.'

The Bible identifies a long list of spiritual gifts (also known as gifts of the Holy Spirit) that God has bestowed on believers. They include administration, discernment, evangelism, healing, hospitality, the word of knowledge, leadership, prophecy, teaching and wisdom, pastoral care, apostleship, mercy, giving, faith (extraordinary trust and surrender) and more. Although several of these sound like natural talents (teaching and administration, for example), others are specific to the lives of believers. I believe Warner Harris is right when he says:

'Talents are developed and expected; gifts are matured and surprising.'

Now, I don't want to give away too much of Session 2! But I'm going to reveal here that I appear to have a talent for leadership – as did my father. Naturally, I learned a great deal from him, through observation and in the course of our many, many discussions and debates . . .

'The art of conversation is the art of hearing as well as of being heard.'
WILLIAM HAZLITT

When I started to mature in my relationship with God, I began to notice I was being mysteriously offered unsolicited opportunities to lead a team or project. As I weighed up these opportunities through prayer and wise counsel, I decided to go for them. It was in working out these opportunities that I discovered I exhibited various leadership skills that were over and above any I might have inherited. For example, somehow (and I firmly believe this skill to be God-given) I was able to get to the heart of a problem and lead a team to a workable solution. I had ideas that (to me) seemed inspired – almost coming out of the blue. These solutions gave me such joy.

AMUSE-BOUCHE

I've watched *MasterChef* a couple of times and, although I'm not in the same league as those talented individuals, I've learned a thing or two from this popular TV show. As you may be aware, the amuse-bouche ('mouth amuser') in exclusive restaurants is a bite-sized portion that is served free, and according to the chef's selection alone. Its purpose is to prepare the guest for the meal and to offer a glimpse of the chef's style.

Drawing on my own experiences, I hope the following sessions will whet your appetite and ignite your desire to discover and use the unique gifts God has given you.

FOR DISCUSSION

1. Have you ever received a gift that completely delighted you, or given one that delighted the recipient? Explain what the gift was and why you feel it evoked such a response.

2. Think of someone you know who has a real gift for something – anything! Are you aware of them using this to glorify God and, if so, in what ways?

3. Do you find it difficult to believe that God has given you a special gift? If so, is this because it's a new idea, or do you feel unworthy of receiving such a blessing? Does it help to imagine the joy God would feel if you responded to what he offers you in love?

SESSION 2
DISCOVERING OUR GIFT AND RESPONDING

WHAT ON EARTH AM I HERE FOR?

Several years ago, I was obsessed with the search to discover my purpose in life and purchased a best-selling book, which guaranteed that after reading and following its prescribed activities, I would do so. I reasoned that identifying my purpose would help me answer one of the greatest of all questions: *What on earth am I here for?* In my efforts to discern what my calling might be, I focused forensically on my life experiences up to that point, seeking clues as to my talents and natural abilities. How enlightened and superior I felt when – after reading the weighty tome, answering its eighty scientifically crafted questions and following the prescribed methodology – I finally produced my very own personal mission statement, perfectly articulating my whole reason for living. What a moment to savour! After many weeks and countless hours of effort, I had reduced my whole life's purpose to a sentence I could recite (on demand if asked) in one breath. All I needed to do then was embody this mission statement so it became my personal rule of life until my dying breath. Job done.

'"I do love it when I am right," Hyacinth said triumphantly. "Which is fortunate, since I so often am."'
JULIA QUINN

With the benefit of (hard-won) insight, I see now that I was driven by a need to be in complete control of my life and how I lived it. While there is nothing inherently wrong with mission statements, personal or otherwise, I was striving to achieve success and significance that was measured by worldly standards, rather than by God's. Eugene Peterson's translation of these New Testament passages is a vivid reminder of the only true and satisfying basis for living:

'We look at this Son and see God's original purpose in everything created. For everything, absolutely everything,

above and below, visible and invisible, rank after rank after rank of angels – *everything* got started in him and finds its purpose in him.'
COLOSSIANS 1:15 (MSG)

'God knew what he was doing from the very beginning. He decided from the outset to shape the lives of those who love him along the same lines as the life of his Son. The Son stands first in the line of humanity he restored. We see the original and intended shape of our lives there in him.'
ROMANS 8:29 (MSG)

My misaligned search had led me to focus on a *purpose* rather than a *person*. I was so preoccupied with determining *what* I should do that I completely missed the simple truth that God's priority centres on *who* I should be in Christ.

Elizabeth Lovell Milford articulates this beautifully:

'Maybe that's truly what discernment is all about; not so much discovering a specific set of actions we are supposed to do, but discovering how to reconnect with God when we are jolted out of a faith lived in auto-pilot, and forced to renew our understanding of purpose.'

Coming to an understanding that our focus should be on Christ and his ongoing, transforming work in our lives not only re-orientates us, but primes us for an adventure of discovery.

'You don't create truth. You find it.'
CRAIG D. LOUNSBROUGH

Discovery is a process; an act of seeing, of gaining information about something previously unknown. God's purpose for the salvation of humankind is inexplicably linked to ourselves. That God would tether himself to us like this, first by way of reconciliation through Christ and then by interweaving his purposes with ours, is an amazing revelation. From the beginning of creation till now – and on to eternity – God walks alongside us through the Holy Spirit, guiding, disciplining and shaping our lives. His mission becomes ours, and ours his. What an unequal partnership. The process of discovery begins with being still . . .

SLOWING DOWN

Being busy has become a status symbol for us in the twenty-first century. We are armed and ready to explain just how short of time we are when asked by our colleagues and friends. It is not for nothing that recent years have seen a proliferation of books, articles and 'how-to' programmes offering methodologies for taming the chaos of daily living and bringing a modicum of order to our existence. Even our smart devices remind us of the necessity to take a minute to be mindful!

'It is not enough to be busy; so are the ants. The question is: What are we busy about?'
HENRY DAVID THOREAU

Yet amid the white noise of ceaseless activity, God gently calls to us to 'be still, and know' (Psalm 46:10). Two crucial questions arise from that verse: What is it to be still? What do I need to know?

Luke 10:38–42 tells the story of Martha and Mary, and provides a salutary lesson in choices and priorities. Partly due to convention, partly to duty, Mary and Martha were both expected to play the role of attentive hostess. The decision Mary made not to undertake the domestic responsibilities expected of her – much to the chagrin of Martha – was vindicated by Jesus' loving judgement on the matter. He welcomed her position (both domestically and physically) and validated her desire for his presence by responding to Martha: 'One thing is needed, and Mary has chosen that good part, which will not be taken away from her' (Luke 10:41–42, NKJV).

'I'd been drowning . . . and flailing on the surface. But what I really needed to do to save myself was let myself sink. It struck me that this is why we say to people, "Calm down." Because beneath the noise of the pounding, swirling surf is a place where all is quiet and clear . . . the chaos stills in this deep.'
GLENNON DOYLE

The season of Lent provides a perfect opportunity to reappraise our priorities. Do we, like Mary, seriously desire to reconnect with God? Are we ready to take up the invitation to draw close and experience his nearness? Time spent in his presence will lead us to deeper levels of 'knowing', and knowledge is the fertile soil in which the ongoing narrative of our lives (our 'doing') is rooted, and subsequently flourishes.

Metaphorically sitting at Jesus' feet, reflecting on and responding to his word, is the one thing that is needed. It demonstrates a countercultural pushback on the unrelenting busyness of our lives.

* * *

Now, you may be wondering what my one-sentence raison d'être turned out to be – and whether it was any help at all in discerning the special gift bestowed on me by God! The answer is both 'yes' and 'no'.

While the exercise usefully pointed me to where my talents, interests and skills lay, its focus was worldly, with no hint of the spiritual and supernatural sphere in which we operate when we encounter the divine. It could not give me the kind of insights I gained from the up-close-and-personal times I spent with God in prayer and reflection. Nor did it allow for the perspectives and wise counsel of loved friends and Christian leaders who knew me, and whose wisdom I treasured.

DISCOVERING OUR GIFT IS NOT A SOLITARY UNDERTAKING

I do recommend that you, too, journey with a close friend or a mature, trusted Christian as you seek what you can be sure is God's desire for you. It is simply this: to be fully engaged in finding out what he desires, 'for it is God who works in you to will and to act in order to fulfil his good purpose' (Philippians 2:13). This includes discerning and discovering his gifts to us.

Matthew 7:7–8 provides a simple framework of possible next steps.

ASK

It may seem so obvious that we miss it(!), but looking to God to help us discern our spiritual gifts is a great place to start.

'If you need wisdom, ask our generous God, and he will give it to you. He will not rebuke you for asking.'
JAMES 1:5 (NLT)

We can pray specifically, patiently and persistently, trusting that our asking pleases God and that he *will* answer our prayers.

It's also important to ask questions of ourselves, and there are several that may be helpful in the gift-discernment process:

- Which topics, news items or injustices concern you, stir you or make you angry?
- What do you do that other people find helpful or encouraging?
- What makes you feel fulfilled and joyful?
- Which endeavours would you be keen to pursue if time or money were no object?
- Which pursuits seem effortless and easy to lose yourself in?

As you answer these questions, be open to the promptings and inner stirrings of the Holy Spirit. God may use different ways to answer your prayer – perhaps through Scripture, perhaps through words of knowledge or 'pictures' from Christians you know and trust. It's useful to write down any apparent answers, so that you can reflect on these at a later time.

SEEK

Just as you would leave no stone unturned in the frantic search for a favoured missing item, be intentional in seeking to discover your spiritual gifts! Request insight and counsel from good friends – people with whom you have shared experiences and spent meaningful time, who know you intimately enough to be clued up about your distinctive traits. Their observations will be valuable on your journey of discovery. Also consider consulting respected Christian leaders such as pastors, clergy, mentors or spiritual directors who may offer a different perspective from that of your close friends. (For example, they may have spent time with you exploring your personality type, using Myers Briggs, the Enneagram, C-me Colour Profiling, or another system.)

Whoever you enlist, I suggest that you ask questions along the following lines:

- What are their impressions of you? What have they noticed about you, your manner and your temperament?
- Is there anything that stands out?
- How would they describe your skills, gifts, talents and so on?
- Where (in their opinion) would your gifts be best deployed, and why?
- Are they available and willing to help you with the next step of finding a safe place to use your gift?

Again, make a note of these conversations so you can reflect on and pray over these later.

Some insights may be unexpected, but they are no less valuable for that. A friend told me, 'My rector suggested I would be well suited to being a eucharistic minister because he discerned a stillness in me. It came as quite a surprise.'

FIND

'Now God gives us many kinds of special abilities, but it is the same Holy Spirit who is the source of them all. There are different kinds of service to God, but it is the same Lord we are serving. There are many ways in which God works in our lives, but it is the same God who does the work in and through all of us who are his.'
1 CORINTHIANS 12:4–6 (TLB)

This next step is where, armed with the reflections, notes, prayers and insights you've gained, you begin to locate the place where your gift may be best used. This will be dependent on the gift you believe you've received from God. For example, if it's hospitality, why not test this by asking him to show you who you might invite for a simple meal at your home? You may wish to pray and plan how you will let them know that God loves them. It may feel appropriate to write an encouraging verse of Scripture on a card and present it at some point during the meal – or maybe God will speak to your guest(s) through your conversation, or simply through the obvious care you have taken to welcome and cook for them.

USING MY SPIRITUAL GIFT

In seeking to find a place to exercise my spiritual gift of leadership, I accepted the invitation to serve on organizing committees and teams, both in church settings and within various community projects. I was also able to draw on the management knowledge gained in my studies, which increased my self-confidence and competence to make sound decisions. Of course, I got some things wrong and was not always pleased with the result. And I'm sure, like many, I suffered from episodic bouts of imposter syndrome. But when I'm operating in my leadership gift, in whatever capacity required, I feel joyful and fulfilled. At times like this, Olympic sprinter and Christian missionary Eric Liddell often comes to my mind. Liddell knew that whenever he was using his God-given gift – running at top speed – God's favour rested on him. His joy was compounded by that of his heavenly Father.

It gives me great joy to lead a team to accomplish a particular project, having developed a strategic plan ready to be implemented, or given advice, or shared a personal vulnerability that is helpful.

FOR DISCUSSION

1. What do you believe your special gift is? If you're not sure, you might make a tentative suggestion and ask others if they feel you're on the right track.

2. Can you think of someone (do change their name for confidentiality reasons if you wish) who has contributed to your growth, or your spiritual or mental well-being, through exercising their special gift? Have you been conscious of a sense of freedom and joy in their lives?

3. Focus on someone in your close circle of Christian friends who may seem quite unaware that they have a spiritual gift. How might you help them recognise and develop this?

SESSION 3
BEING WITH JESUS AND BECOMING FRUITFUL

COME WITH ME: MATTHEW 4:19

I imagine when Jesus invited Peter and his brother Andrew to embark on a new adventure in Matthew 4:19, it was quite a challenge. '"Come, follow me," Jesus said, "and I will send you out to fish for people."' I've always been intrigued by Mathew's account in verse 20: 'At once they left their nets and followed him.' This gives the impression that they immediately downed tools. However, we learn in John 1:35–42 that these men were already acquainted with Jesus (he had earlier renamed Simon 'Peter'). Having spent time observing him and hearing him preach and teach, they were convinced, when the invitation came, that following Jesus would change their lives forever.

'When you are loved well, you want more of it. The only reason I believe anyone would not desire to be a disciple of Christ is because they fail to realize just how well loved they are by him. How could you not want to be with someone who loves you well?'
SANDRA M. MICHELLE

We're no different from those humble fishermen, in that saying 'yes' to Jesus signals the beginning of a life of exploration and discovery. For three years the disciples ate, slept, observed, travelled, debated and served with Jesus. (They also sometimes rubbed one another up the wrong way and quarrelled about who was the greatest!) We, too, encounter Jesus in and through the circumstances and complexities of our everyday existence. And yet, two thousand years on, our world has become, in some ways, a much more complex place. Law firm founder Chad Causey states:

'The degree of hyper-connectedness in our world has changed every job, every industry and every market.'

When the Covid-19 pandemic struck in early 2020, commentators speculated that one effect might be to fast-track us to a better world. Political, social and economic divides would be lessened as we were encouraged to take a more compassionate view of ourselves and those around us. However, for many communities in the UK and elsewhere, the potential benefits have not materialised. Eighteen months on, we can breathe a sigh of relief that the constraints on our freedoms have been lifted and we can re-enter society to pick up where we left off. But we have been unwilling participants in a life-changing and potentially traumatic experience. Our post-Covid-19 landscape may seem familiar, but scars of grief, isolation and loss have wrought havoc on the mental health of many, causing some to turn inwards and others to seek new adrenaline-fuelled experiences, simply to feel alive.

It is in this muddled, messy society that God calls, empowers and gifts us to become people of influence for his glory. This is both scary and superb. We might wonder: how can we – ordinary, flawed human beings – be trusted with God's stuff? Yet, dear friends, he has every confidence! He has equipped us and partnered with us, to see his kingdom come. We are reminded in 2 Corinthians 4:7 that:

'We have this treasure in earthen vessels, that the excellence of the power may be of God and not of us' (NKJV).

This should bring comfort and reassurance, because we know it is God, through his Spirit, who is at work in us. And because of that fact, we can kick our fear of failure to the curb. Wherever Christians work, reside, holiday or visit, that place becomes the habitation of the Holy Spirit and fertile ground for transformation.

'The gifts and callings God places inside us are irrevocable, and there is no force on earth or in heaven that could come against or stop His love.'
KIM WALKER-SMITH

At the beginning of his ministry, Jesus moved from his hometown of Nazareth to live in Capernaum, twenty miles further north.

Commentators speculate that the reason for this relocation was so that he could have an impact on the greatest number of people, as Capernaum was a much busier city than Nazareth. His move fulfilled the prophecy of Isaiah 9:1–2, which states that the Messiah would be a light to that region. The presence and proximity of Jesus illuminated a dark place and drew people to engage with Immanuel, God who is *with us*.

Every day, we have the opportunity to reflect on Jesus' mission, to:

'Let your light shine before others, that they may see your good deeds and glorify your Father in heaven.'
MATTHEW 5:16

BECOMING FRUITFUL

The Bible often uses the metaphor of fruit to describe the produce of our lives – either good or bad. We are called to fruitfulness, not only when we are at church or in our home groups, but wherever we spend significant hours of our day. This may not sit comfortably with our mindset. We are often unwittingly persuaded to assume that success in life is ultimately reliant upon the individual – their hard work, application and the risks they are willing to take. In other words, to be successful and get everything we want in life, we are responsible for charting our course and navigating all the obstacles that obscure our path.

This philosophy contrasts with how the Bible commends dependency and reliance on God. Jesus modelled this dependence to his disciples. The verse, 'he can do only what he sees his Father doing' (John 5:19), describes the intimate relationship he had with the Father: one of perfect unity, obedience and yielding. Here success is measured by an entirely different currency.

Mark Greene writes in his book, *Fruitfulness on the Frontline*:

'As we live in step with the Spirit, God's glory radiates out through who we are in him, what we do and say in his

power, like light beaming from the facets of a diamond . . .
Fruitfulness is not an end in itself . . . [it] is intended to point
to the wonder of the Father.'

A normal day may feel ordinary. It may be good, bad or just
about survivable. But God is present with us on that day. We are
present (for large parts of each twenty-four hours) with others,
too, whether in offices, factories, hospitals, gyms, supermarkets,
hairdressers or stadia, and we can be sure that he will provide
opportunities for us to be the bearers of his grace and beacons of
transformation.

'A kind gesture can reach a wound that only compassion
can heal.'
STEVE MARABOLI

Jesus highlights, in his teaching about the vine and the branches,
a direct correlation between dependency or reliance on him
('abiding') and fruitfulness.

'I am the true vine, and my Father is the gardener . . .
Remain in me, as I also remain in you. No branch can bear
fruit by itself; it must remain in the vine. Neither can you
bear fruit unless you remain in me . . . This is to my Father's
glory, that you bear much fruit, showing yourselves to be
my disciples.'
JOHN 15:1–8

Fruitfulness is the by-product of an intimate relationship with Christ.
He alone is the source of all that we need to grow and flourish.
As branches cling to the vine, so we are encouraged to cling to
Christ, drawing our very life from him. The Father's goal is for us
to produce 'much fruit' as he uses our gifts to bring blessing to a
broken world.

TURNING ON A SIXPENCE

To 'turn on a sixpence' is an old-fashioned idiom conveying
an individual's ability to act quickly or with agile precision.
As radiographers in the NHS, the robust clinical training my

colleagues and I received (like all who hold patient-facing roles in the health sector) included being ready, at a moment's notice, to deploy life-saving measures. The moment an emergency arose, every person in the vicinity was either actively engaged or awaiting instruction from the senior medic in attendance. This was no time to show indecision or incompetence, but rather to nerve yourself to undertake the tasks assigned to you.

'Keep your fears to yourself, but share your courage with others.'
ROBERT LOUIS STEVENSON

Similarly, God's gifts prepare us for dynamic involvement in the world wherever and whenever he calls us to engage. If we truly believe that God longs for every single person on earth to hear the good news of salvation, hope and transformation, then his mission is only possible when every Christian is prepared to speak or act sensitively, relevantly and confidently.

During our medical training, a fellow student and I found ourselves at a loose end. The waiting room was empty, with no patients booked in for X-rays. Out of the blue, my colleague asked me about my faith. Did being a Christian make a difference to my life and the things I chose to do? Aware that our boss was seated in an adjacent room and could overhear our conversation, I hesitated in answering him. Yet I felt compelled to share my story there and then, and it didn't take long to do so. I know that my testimony made a difference to David that day. How? Because not many weeks afterwards, when offered the invitation, he gave his life to Christ.

Using our gifts does not always yield such obvious results. Indeed, the fruit of our ministry may not be seen for many weeks, years or even within our lifetime. But through obedience to God, we become our authentic selves, using our gifts to make Christ known wherever we serve. Fruitfulness for those committed to Christ is to be alert to the significance of our presence, as partners in God's mission, within our sphere of influence.

St Francis de Sales (1567–1622) is recorded as saying this while he was Bishop of Geneva:

'Truly charity has no limit; for the love of God has been poured into our hearts by His Spirit dwelling in each one of us, calling us to a life of devotion and inviting us to bloom in the garden where He has planted and directing us to radiate the beauty and spread the fragrance of His Providence.'

And to return to Mark Greene:

'Our attitudes and our actions, our work and our words . . . [should include] a concern for the individuals we meet and for the organizations, families and nations we are part of . . . the culture we are in.'

FOR DISCUSSION

1. When have you been particularly conscious of Jesus' presence with you? Do you have a sense of him as a companion and friend?

2. Are there people who seem Christlike to you? Explain why this might be so.

3. Choose a recent day. Can you think of a moment of grace when God was clearly working through you or others?

SESSION 4
WHEN THINGS GO WRONG, AND WAYS OF STAYING ON TRACK

'THE GRASS IS GREENER' SYNDROME

Hands up if you have ever heard of 'GIGS'. No, I hadn't heard of it either, but GIGS is a thing! It stands for 'grass is greener syndrome' and may, for example, describe a scenario where one person leaves a seemingly great situation or relationship because they (mistakenly) believe that something or someone else would be better than what they are currently experiencing. As we explored in Session 1, the tendency towards constant comparison, which often goes alongside an inability to be grateful and appreciative of the gifts and abilities we possess, is one we must be alert to, though this is certainly not easy – especially when social media platforms suggest that everyone else is excelling in life . . . except you!

'Define yourself radically as one beloved by God. This is the true self. Every other identity is illusion.'
BRENNAN MANNING

You should expect to go through times of uncertainty and insecurity, particularly when you're moving through the phases of discovering, discerning and deploying your special gift. However, an unrelenting focus on comparing yourself with others is a disastrous exercise. As Theodore Roosevelt famously said: 'Comparison is the thief of joy.' Don't let your joy be stolen!

'Peter must have thought, "Who am I compared to Mr. Faithfulness (John)?" But Jesus clarified the issue. John was responsible for John. Peter was responsible for Peter. And each had only one command to heed: "Follow Me."'
CHARLES R. SWINDOLL

In common with many Christians, I've been fighting a running battle with GIGS for most of my adult life. I have no trouble at all in identifying individuals I deem to be much more capable than I am! Helpfully, the Bible urges us to be mindful of this comparison trap (Galatians 6:4–5 and 2 Corinthians 10:12), because indulging in it leads us towards unfruitfulness, ineffectiveness and stagnation. How then might we prepare ourselves for the 'you versus me', comparison-focused mind battles we encounter? Or for those barren seasons when we doubt our fruitfulness? There are two primary truths that I believe may be helpful.

The first truth we need to take hold of is that, as fallen human beings, we have a natural inclination to sin. Left to our own devices, and regardless of the veracity of our willpower, it will not be long before we fail. This is because we have an enemy, Satan, for whom we are easy prey. 1 Peter 5:8 warns us:

'Be alert and of sober mind. Your enemy the devil prowls around like a roaring lion looking for someone to devour.'

However, as Christians, our status has changed. Through Christ's saving work on the cross, we are now redeemed human beings. God is not only our Creator; he is also our Father, and good fathers look after their families. So, God does not leave us alone or unprotected against the onslaught of the enemy. Scripture testifies that he has:

'Granted to us everything pertaining to life and godliness, through the true knowledge of Him who called us by His own glory and excellence.'
2 PETER 1:3 (NASB)

The more we possess a true knowledge of God, the more accessible his provisions for us become. Further, grounding ourselves in his word helps us to become more aware of Satan's techniques – including the lure of comparing ourselves with each other. As Nicky Gumbel says:

'If the grass looks greener on the other side, it is probably astroturf!'

We may well smile, but there is a subtle truth lurking within this entertaining observation. Rationally, we know that each of us has struggles of some kind, but it is difficult to assimilate this knowledge if we constantly allow ourselves to believe that we are life's second-rate citizens.

'God creates out of nothing. Wonderful, you say. Yes, to be sure, but he does what is still more wonderful: he makes saints out of sinners.'
SØREN KIERKEGAARD

The second truth for us to hold to is the knowledge that God *always* works in, with and through us.

GOD WORKING IN US

'For it is God who works in you, both to will and to work for his good pleasure.'
PHILIPPIANS 2:13 (ESV)

Jesus submitted his whole life, thought, word and deed to the will of his Father, choosing day by day to walk in step with the Holy Spirit. It is vitally important that we do not seek to do good works in our own strength. As believers, indwelt and led by the Holy Spirit, we must choose to submit our lives to him daily and ask him to make us willing co-partners.

GOD WORKING WITH US

'For we are fellow workers in God's service; you are God's field, God's building.'
1 CORINTHIANS 3:9

As bearers of God's image, he created us for worship and intimacy with himself. But he has also bestowed dignity and purpose on us by equipping us to share in his mission to humankind.

GOD WORKING THROUGH US

'I can do all things through Christ who strengthens me.'
PHILIPPIANS 4:13 (NKJV)

Following Jesus is a choice we make over and over again. Our discipleship will no doubt lead us into unfamiliar and challenging situations and circumstances. We may feel ill-equipped to deal with these, but it is in and through the difficulties that we learn to trust him and rest in the knowledge that he alone is God and we are not. God is in control at all times, and there is never, ever a time that we are forsaken or unprotected.

'I will have nothing to do with a God who cares only occasionally. I need a God who is with us always, everywhere, in the deepest depths as well as the highest heights. It is when things go wrong, when good things do not happen, when our prayers seem to have been lost, that God is most present. We do not need the sheltering wings when things go smoothly. We are closest to God in the darkness, stumbling along blindly.'
MADELEINE L'ENGLE

WE ALL NEED EACH OTHER

One of my favourite songs is an old soulful classic, 'We All Need Each Other', by Danniebelle Hall.[1] Although we instinctively know and subscribe to this truth, it is necessary to remind ourselves continuously that we thrive by being dependent upon one another. So far, we have focused on the gifts and fruitfulness of the individual. But the church community – that glorious mosaic of diverse individuals – is the primary place for the functioning of gifts and fruit to be demonstrated. It is within the community of Jesus' followers that gifts are discerned, tested and matured – all to the glory of God.

It is sad therefore when the Church seems to suggest there is a hierarchy of charismatic gifts, heralding some and devaluing others. This was the situation that existed in Corinth, where some Christians were grumbling that their Spirit-given gift wasn't valuable or visible enough. Paul addresses this major misunderstanding head-on using the analogy of the body and its many vital, integrated parts, whether seen or unseen.

[1] You can listen to 'We All Need Each Other' here: <https://www.youtube.com/watch?v=oS3yfwN6ikk>.

'The eye cannot say to the hand, "I don't need you!" And
the head cannot say to the feet, "I don't need you!" On the
contrary, those parts of the body that seem to be weaker
are indispensable, and the parts that we think are less
honourable we treat with special honour. And the parts that
are unpresentable are treated with special modesty, while
our presentable parts need no special treatment. But God
has put the body together, giving greater honour to the parts
that lacked it, so that there should be no division in the body,
but that its parts should have equal concern for each other.'
1 CORINTHIANS 12:21–25

By contrast, *all* the spiritual gifts, working as God envisages them,
are essential for the proper functioning of a local church, thereby
building up the body of Christ (Ephesians 4:12–13).

THE CHALLENGE OF BEING FRUITFUL IN NON-CHURCH SETTINGS

The Great Commission (Matthew 28:16–20) is a full-time
occupation; it was never envisaged as the exclusive preserve of
ordained ministers alone. Numerically, I'd warrant that couldn't
possibly stack up, given the ratio of ordained ministers to those yet
to be reached with the good news. As I keep mentioning, for the
Great Commission to be completed, *every* follower of Jesus must be
unswervingly committed and intentionally engaged in its fulfilment.

Is there a tendency to segment our lives into spiritual and
non-spiritual elements? As we saw in the last session, how we
operate in so-called secular spaces is important too! Being slow
to recognise this – or afraid to take risks – may well result in us
missing opportunities to use our gifts within the sphere of influence
where we spend the greatest proportion of our time.

'God doesn't call us to be comfortable. He calls us to trust
Him so completely that we are unafraid to put ourselves in
situations where we will be in trouble if He doesn't come
through.'
FRANCIS CHAN

'Don't worry about other people's opinions of you. God never told you to impress people; only to love them.'
DAVE WILLIS

That said, being in a non-church environment, especially a work-based one, can understandably militate against our evangelical efforts, especially where there's a threat of a legal case being brought against us. However, authentic colleague relationships and friendships may well provide favourable circumstances to use our gifts openly, sensitively and appropriately.

YOU DON'T HAVE TO ASK ME TWICE!

My NHS colleagues knew I was a person of faith. Now and then, individuals would ask the odd question about the Church or God, and I would answer as best I could. Just before Easter one year, the chair of the social committee approached me. She tentatively explained that she suspected there was more to Easter than she thought, but she wasn't quite sure what it was. It couldn't simply be about fluffy bunnies and chocolate eggs, could it? Would I be at all interested in sharing the true meaning of Easter with my colleagues?

Well, dear reader, she didn't need to ask me twice! I said I would love the opportunity – and I went for it. I commandeered some gospel singers, called in favours from a couple of musicians, and prepared a three-minute talk about Jesus' death and resurrection, and what this means for every individual. I had my colleagues' undivided attention for twenty minutes before the glut of Easter eggs was eventually dispensed.

I often think about this unique opportunity. Despite being firmly out of my comfort zone, I recognised God working through the situation. He was present right there, in my workplace, perfectly at home amid the desks, PCs and water coolers.

'Sometimes I arrive just when God's ready to have someone click the shutter.'
ANSEL ADAMS

Interestingly, I wasn't asked to speak again the following year!
You may never get the same opportunity twice, but you can
be sure that whatever you do as a co-worker with God, the
adventure you embark on will be a glorious one.

FOR DISCUSSION

1. How do you cope with negative thoughts, such as feeling
others are more competent than you, or that your life would be
happier in different circumstances? Are you aware of techniques
that might help you intervene when these feelings arise?

2. When do you feel most yourself? Is it when you're involved in
a particular work or leisure activity, or when you're with a certain
person or people, or in other circumstances?

3. Looking over the past year, can you identify a time when you
were working in harmony with other people and achieved an
outcome that was glorifying to God?

SESSION 5
IT'S ALL GOOD – HOW GOD CHANGES EVERYTHING

IN THE BEGINNING

In the beginning God created the heavens and the earth. Now the earth was formless and empty, darkness was over the surface of the deep, and the Spirit of God was hovering over the waters.

And God said, 'Let there be light,' and there was light. God saw that the light was good, and he separated the light from the darkness.

So God created mankind in his own image,
    in the image of God he created them;
    male and female he created them.

God blessed them and said to them, 'Be fruitful and increase in number; fill the earth and subdue it.'

God saw all that he had made, and it was very good.
GENESIS 1:1–4, 27–28, 31

God had a plan from the very start, and it always included humankind. His overwhelming love for us and his desire to deliver us from evil culminated in the precious gift of his son. God revealed, through Christ's sacrificial death and resurrection, his gift of salvation, calling us 'out of darkness into his marvellous light' (1 Peter 2:9). Just as the Holy Spirit hovered over the face of a formless and empty void, so today he hovers over humankind, stirring our hearts in the hope of bringing us to birth as his new creation. Thanks be to God for his indescribable gift (2 Corinthians 9:15).

As I said earlier, this would have been enough! But God bestows spiritual gifts on those who have received him; gifts that empower believers to meet the needs of the Church and beyond for his glory.

'I would rather be what God chose to make me than the most glorious creature that I could think of; for to have been thought about, born in God's thought, and then made by God, is the dearest, grandest and most precious thing in all thinking.'
GEORGE MACDONALD

The body of Christ is strengthened and the kingdom of Christ is brought near in every place a believer occupies. This is fruitfulness indeed; not only to serve those who worship along with us, but to express worship through our service in our communities in the 'wonderful everyday'. If that phrase seems familiar, let me remind you it is the slogan masterfully engineered by IKEA to make people think about its brand while subliminally planting in our minds the enticing idea that we will come closer to living our best, most productive lives if we simply buy their stuff. For those empowered by the Holy Spirit, there is so much more!

'What you are is God's gift to you, what you become is your gift to God.'
HANS URS VON BALTHASAR

HIS PRESENCE CHANGES EVERYTHING

I remember very well the day I came to faith. I was a teenager, and reluctantly accepted an invitation to a 'revival meeting'. Long story short, when the evangelist issued the invitation to 'come to Jesus', somehow (I don't remember how) I ran to the front of the church and there I had an encounter. It was as though a bright, warm light were shining into the dark and empty void of my soul, renewing, restoring and reconciling me to God. That was a life-transforming moment because I knew, without a shadow of a doubt, that I was standing in his presence.

As we have been exploring, our conversion is something that is of far greater benefit than simply a personal experience. John Stott, a noted leader of the worldwide evangelical movement, wrote:

'Social responsibility becomes an aspect not of Christian mission only, but also of Christian conversion. It is impossible to be truly converted to God without being thereby converted to our neighbour.'

Perhaps that insight is of some relevance to this little story. There is a song that has had a powerful impact on me ever since I first heard it many years ago. It is 'The Heart of Worship' by Matt Redman.[2] Matt describes the context for the penning of this song:

'There was a dynamic missing, so the pastor did a pretty brave thing. He decided to get rid of the sound system and band for a season, and we gathered together with just our voices. His point was that we'd lost our way in worship, and the way to get back to the heart would be to strip everything away.'

The congregation's response was to sing their songs a cappella, and in doing so – accompanied by heartfelt prayers – they freshly encountered God.

The song reminds me that I am easily distracted. How do I, as Matt invokes in his song, learn to strip away the non-essentials to discover the most valuable treasure of all? The journey from Lent to Easter invites us on a personal pilgrimage where we – like Mary choosing presence over domesticity – draw close to Jesus once again. It's all about you, Jesus. My prayer is that I, too, will choose the better part that will not be taken away from me.

THE GLORY OF EASTER AND NEW BEGINNINGS

'Therefore, if anyone is in Christ, he is a new creation; old things have passed away; behold, all things have become new.'
2 CORINTHIANS 5:17 (NKJV)

[2] You can watch and listen to a lyric version of 'The Heart of Worship' here: <https://www.youtube.com/watch?v=gljs4N7ZoD4>.

For Christians, Easter is a glorious time, symbolising, as it does, new beginnings and victory over death. Even as we struggle through the forty days of Lent, in reflection and repentance, we are conscious of God's love for us – so poignantly articulated by John in his Gospel:

'For God so loved the world that he gave his one and only Son, that whoever believes in him shall not perish but have eternal life.'
JOHN 3:16

And John would know, having been distinguished as 'the disciple whom Jesus loved' (John 13:23). Significantly different from Matthew, Mark and Luke, his Gospel begins with the profound announcement that Jesus was 'in the beginning', and ends with the commissioning of Peter, a man desperately broken by his denial of Jesus. Only weeks before, Peter had boldly proclaimed Jesus as Lord and Messiah, and sworn his allegiance to him. In this encounter, on the shores of Lake Galilee where Jesus had first called Peter to follow him, Jesus imbues Peter with a new beginning and a new story.

'What makes authentic disciples is not visions, ecstasies, biblical mastery of chapter and verse, or spectacular success in the ministry, but a capacity for faithfulness. Buffeted by the fickle winds of failure, battered by their own unruly emotions, and bruised by rejection and ridicule, authentic disciples may have stumbled and frequently fallen, endured lapses and relapses, gotten handcuffed to the fleshpots and wandered into a far county. Yet, they kept coming back to Jesus.'
BRENNAN MANNING

That new beginning was not his alone. All the disciples would have been profoundly impacted by Jesus' crucifixion. Forty days after his resurrection, Luke tells us, they followed his instructions to wait in Jerusalem, and we can only imagine how their lives changed in that time, as they reflected on their three-year apprenticeship. Every encounter, healing and teaching must have been replayed and reviewed, surely leading them to see Jesus with new eyes – not as their rabbi, but as the risen Lord, Messiah and King. All that had gone before had been leading up to this moment of clarity. Doubt was replaced by the solid conviction that they had good news to share, for the Scriptures indicate that the empowering of the disciples by the Holy Spirit catapulted them into demonstrating the power of the gospel to transform lives in the same way theirs had been just a few years earlier.

'But you will receive power when the Holy Spirit comes on you; and you will be my witnesses in Jerusalem, and in all Judea and Samaria, and to the ends of the earth.'
ACTS 1:8

C. S. Lewis wrote, 'There are far, far better things ahead than any we leave behind.' John's description in his Gospel of forgiveness, reconciliation and renewal is also our personal story. And not only that: we too are assigned by God to become the catalysts of reconciliation.

'Therefore, if anyone is in Christ, the new creation has come: the old has gone, the new is here! All this is from God, who reconciled us to himself through Christ and gave us the ministry of reconciliation: that God was reconciling the world to himself in Christ, not counting people's sins against them. And he has committed to us the message of reconciliation.'
2 CORINTHIANS 5:17–19

As his co-workers, we are deployed beyond the walls of our churches, through the outworking of our gifts, to claim every space we inhabit as a sacred place of divine encounter and renewal.

'I once listened to an Indian on television say that God was in the wind and the water, and I wondered at how beautiful that was because it meant you could swim in Him or have Him brush your face in a breeze.'
DONALD MILLER

THAT WOW MOMENT

What I described in Session 1 actually started as an 'ouch' moment! My diary entry at that time reveals that I was burned out and comprehensively exhausted by the sheer burden of my duties and responsibilities. Imperceptibly, I'd become untethered from the spiritual disciplines that had preserved my closeness and dependency on Jesus, so I did not recognise the encroaching barrenness that stole my joy. However, as the recipient of overwhelming generosity and effusive hospitality, slowly, over that week, I was revived and renewed. Darkness gave way to light.

In this season of Lent, let's recognise that a new beginning from God is one of his most amazing gifts to us. It offers an opportunity for growth, transformation and maturity. Yet it is not a gift for us alone, for we are commissioned – like Peter and the disciples before us – to play our part in spreading the good news of God's saving love, all over the world.

'God has given a spiritual gift to the church in you, and you dare not keep it to yourself.'
AARON NIEQUIST

FOR DISCUSSION

1. Having completed this course, do you, as a person 'born in God's thought' (as George MacDonald puts it), have a clearer idea of who he is calling you to be?

2. Can you think of a time when you (or someone you know) were burned out or exhausted, and then suddenly found yourself the recipient of overwhelming and unexpected blessing?

3. How might you use your special God-given gift for his glory this week?

TRANSCRIPT
INTRODUCTION

OLIVIA   Hello. I'm Olivia Amartey, and welcome to this York Course, *The Gift of Christ*. I'm joined by two lovely people, and I'm going to let them introduce themselves.

PAUL   Hello, I'm Paul Kerensa. I'm a comedian, a writer, a broadcaster and, most importantly, a human being, bumbling his way through life [*Olivia laughs*] and making the best of it.

OLIVIA   Like me!

AMY   And I'm Amy Boucher Pye. I'm a writer, a speaker, a retreat leader, a spiritual director and God's beloved. How pretentious does that sound?

PAUL   And quite right too – own it!

AMY   But you guys are as well. [*Olivia laughs.*] Oh, did you hear my Minnesotan come out, 'you guys'? Sorry, Olivia! [*Olivia laughs.*]

OLIVIA   No, that's OK! You're both very welcome. As are you. And we look forward to seeing you in Session 1.

SESSION 1
THE GENEROSITY OF GOD

OLIVIA Hello, welcome to Session 1: The generosity of God. And Paul, I'd like to start with you. Have you ever received a gift that completely delighted you, or given one that delighted the recipient?

PAUL Well, I think for me, it's a case of the really personal, and the one that you just can't plan, you stumble into. And I'm instantly cast back to being in a theme park in Holland, of all places, with my wife and my kids. And I was distracting my children by taking them into a thing . . . I couldn't understand what it was, it was a booth of some sort, like a passport photo booth? And they stepped in. And my children were like 5 and 6, and this camera all around suddenly appeared and we stepped back going, *What was that?* And a bit of paper appeared at the end of it, saying we have now taken a three-dimensional photograph of your children! And I walked back going, *What is this exactly?* And then I emailed the thing and it came back and it said, we will now print for you, if you would like to, if you want to spend the £30 or whatever, this little model of your children. And I had absolutely no idea what I was walking into. But that Christmas, I gave my wife these two little models of our kids and they're still on our mantelpiece to this day. It's a little bit weird, but [*Olivia laughs*] we stumbled into it, going into this situation, going, *What in the world are we doing here?* But it was personal, it was improvised, and it was off the cuff and you couldn't plan it. But we had our eyes open to it and it went down well.

OLIVIA Now Amy, [let's] turn to you. What does the generosity of God mean to you?

AMY Well, God is such a generous giver, isn't he? And I love how when we have our eyes open, as you said, Paul, we can see the gifts that are around us. I mean a random 3-D portrait of your kid [*everyone laughs*], who would have thought? But God is in the everyday because he's the most generous, because he created us, he formed us and he gave us Jesus, and he redeems us, and he saves us, and he fills us with love. He is so generous; not only in the grand, huge, massive ways, but in the everyday of opening up our eyes to such a wonderful gift that you received and that you were able to give to your wife that . . . has a prized place on the mantelpiece. I love that!

OLIVIA   That's great. And Paul, if you're thinking about the generosity of God in your own life, how do you channel the generosity of God in your life? How do you see it working and playing out?

PAUL   . . . It's a constant sort of trying to get back on that path, I think, to make sure that we're doing that. And I made a few conscious decisions over the last few years to try and be more generous – not just in terms of money, but of time, of energy, of attention and focus. And if I'm asked for a commendation, or can you recommend me for something, rather than just do a quick version, go, 'Well, I'm busy, I'm doing this.' . . . We always think we're so busy doing this, that, the other. Instead, I'm realising that, actually, if you go above and beyond, it really is rewarding, not just for yourself, but for the other people. And suddenly, they go, 'Wow, I did not expect that. I didn't.' . . . If you go above and beyond and go, 'You know, I'm not just going to do you a quick version of that. I'll do you the best version I possibly can,' it's really appreciated. And suddenly, you make those connections with people. Any of those acts of generosity that forms a greater human connection, I think is all part of God's masterwork, I'm sure.

OLIVIA   Yeah, I was just thinking about what you were just saying there, Paul. I was thinking about generosity as well. I mean, when we think of generosity, I think oftentimes we think about generosity as being something that somebody gives us, or that we want to be generous with somebody else. But I've – perhaps it's just getting older [laughs] maybe – but, for me, generosity's around time – the fact that someone will give me their time. And that I can spare time. So, it's not always about a gift that I may give someone or something that somebody may give to me, but it's about the time that I spend with them. And I don't know if that's a sign of old age or whatever, but I find that having time is probably the most important thing for me, and giving my time as well is also important. I don't know what you may think about that, Amy? What do you think about how you've seen the generosity of God play out in your life?

AMY   Yeah. Well, you say the gift of time. It's interesting when you hear about some of these love languages, and one of them is the gift of time.

OLIVIA   Yes. Yeah.

AMY   And one of our kids, that is the love language of this child. And I tend to be probably too driven and too project-oriented, and I have to go, 'Oh,' and so I say, 'I really want to spend time with you,' and it's a reminder to myself, and it's also pouring out generosity on a person that I do want to spend time with. It's one of my kids, you know. Whereas my love language is gifts, which can be kind of embarrassing because it's not that I want you to shower me with gifts! You know, I don't really want your 3-D thingy anyway, sorry! [*Paul and Olivia laugh.*] But I want to know that you know me. So, like, if you find a gift that says, you know, something about writing or spirituality or whatever, it's finding a gift where, 'Oh my word, I just came across this most amazing thing because I know you will love it!'

OLIVIA   Yes.

AMY   You don't know you need it, but you do because it says that *I see you*. And I think the generosity of God fills us, and we give back in ways that we like to express. And there are all these different ways of showing love and receiving love.

OLIVIA   I certainly want to be your friend, that's for sure. [*Everyone laughs.*]

AMY   Definitely.

OLIVIA   That's great. Paul, you're a sitcom writer, and I'm sure there are other things that you do well too. But tell us a little bit about that gift and how you use that.

PAUL   I think sitcom writing is one of those things that it's hard work when you're doing it, in a way. I like having written rather than the actual process of writing, because it's very tricky to get all those threads together. But the rewards of it are just so wonderful, that I hadn't really fully appreciated until we first started writing for sitcoms like Miranda Hart's show, which really connected with people on a different level, I think. Because I've had people then quote bits back to me years, a decade later, even. An actress I worked with recently who was in her mid-twenties and she said to me, she said, 'Oh, I used to watch *Miranda* growing up.' I thought, *Oh, now I feel old, suddenly!* [*Olivia laughs.*] And she was quoting back to me a line that I'd written fifteen years earlier or something like that.

OLIVIA   Tell us the line, Paul.

PAUL   I can't remember it exactly [*Olivia and Amy laugh*], and I'd probably have to pay royalties as well . . . but it was just wonderful to realise that actually some of those silly ideas that you have in front of a laptop end up getting into people's consciousness and giving that sense of a lift of joy, you know, a sense of happiness and a sense of . . . especially if you can get those things that I think as a comedy writer we're all trying to reach for, which we don't really land on too often, which are those things that unite people and give people a better, more elevated, more godly view of the world, I think, as opposed to being down on the world. You know, we need uplift, we need lifting up, and I think that [it's] not just comedy writing, but we can do that in our lives as well. Because the thing is, it's a very solitary, you know, you're writing from home, but we can use that same process, that same idea, the same concept of being in a café, a pub, you know, out with friends and trying to lift them where they are, and it's that same idea, I think.

OLIVIA   And how wonderful . . .

AMY   How the world would be a different place if we were all doing that! Sorry, I just had to burst in when you think about how the world is.

OLIVIA   I know, I was thinking . . . absolutely.

PAUL   Well, it's the same thing, especially with comedians and comedy writers, there's that thing of punching down or punching up. You know, do you want to sort of pick on the little people or do you want to actually say, 'Look we can all raise our game, raise the bar and raise a bit of happiness and joy'? And I don't do it often enough. I'm saying it like I do this. I don't do it all the time, but it's a great aim, I think, and I need to do it more myself, certainly.

OLIVIA   . . . What a wonderful gift to be able to give the world joy through laughter. Isn't that great? And Amy, you're a writer. Tell us a little bit about your gift and how you use that.

AMY   Well, it always feels a bit cringy to talk about . . .

OLIVIA   What *inspires* you?

AMY   . . . one's gift, doesn't it? But I love seeing where God is at work. I love the Bible. I love the richness of the Bible and I'm a spiritual director. So, I love to see how God is at work in your life. I mean, 'spiritual direction' is such an archaic term. It's really accompanying people on their spiritual journey, noticing where God is at work in their life, helping *them* to notice. And so, I love leading people into encountering God. That's why I love prayer and prayer exercises . . . So it's seeing God at work because he is; he's so involved in our lives. So, empowering people to see the way that he changes them, and leading them to encountering God just makes me really happy.

OLIVIA   Amy, thank you so much for that. And so that brings us to the end of Session 1. I really look forward to being with you for Session 2.

SESSION 2
DISCOVERING OUR GIFT AND RESPONDING

OLIVIA   Hello, welcome to Session 2: Discovering our gift and responding. Just going to jump straight in there and ask you a question, Amy. So how did you discover your gift?

AMY   Well, it was a long journey, as these things usually are. I always wanted to be a writer. And in fact, when I was in the fourth grade, which is like Year 3 in the UK, I had a short story published in the *Minneapolis Star*. And yes, you might think that it was this, you know, straightforward journey from that tender young age. But no, there were many different hoops and jumps, and all those kinds of things that I'm slaughtering, even now, those words. But it was a journey of finding out who I was in God, as God's beloved, and that I could own being a writer, that I could own having something to say, because God had created me and gave me things to say. So I didn't turn out to be a writer for many, many, many years. I was an editor and I'm not saying that all editors are wannabe writers. They're not. It's a wonderful profession. But for me, it was, I didn't feel like I could be a writer because I didn't have anything to say. So, I edited other people's things. But then slowly, slowly, slowly, over seven years I wrote my first book, which never got published (thankfully!) [*Olivia laughs*], and I stepped into the identity and it was part of that imposter syndrome of, I'm a writer. But then you start saying it and doing it and then you realise . . . And I'm so much more than just a writer, you know. I'm God's beloved.

OLIVIA   Absolutely. I mean I resonate with your story there. As a classic introvert, the only thing that I felt I could do when I was younger was to write. So it was the only way I thought I could really express myself and my thoughts to God, especially when I became a Christian. So I understand some of that there. And when you say that you're a writer, you do certainly feel kind of pompous, doesn't it, in many ways?

AMY   It does! Yes!

OLIVIA   But it's about expressing the gift that God gives, isn't it? It's so good. Thank you for sharing that. Paul, I'm going to come to you with a really tough question.

PAUL   OK.

OLIVIA   On a day-to-day basis, how strong is your desire to feel as if you're in control of your life?

PAUL   Oh my word!

OLIVIA   Told you it's a tough question.

PAUL   It is a tough question, especially because you think the *desire* to feel . . . I *desire* it, certainly. Do I *feel* it? Sometimes, but I know full well, particularly those sort of crossroads moments in my life where you . . . it's a bit of a cliché, isn't it, the crossroads moments. You think, *Which way shall I turn? Shall I go left? Shall I go right?* But so often we're sort of slightly jostled in one direction or the other. And it does feel like we're taking a journey where we think, I'm going to set out on that motorway and I'm going to go at this speed. And then, of course, there's a road closure, there's a diversion, there's cars, you know, pushing you into that lane and the other.

And I look at those major moments in my life and in my career, and similarly to Amy, you know, I started out thinking I quite liked . . . and I wanted to be a writer, I wanted to be an actor. I had no idea, I ended up doing a bit of radio and a bit of this and a bit of that, a bit of TV, sitcom writing, where did that come from? And all of those are just those moments of meeting the right person, being in the right place at the right time.

OLIVIA   Yes.

PAUL   My first ever sitcom writing job I got with Lee Mack, you know, well-known comedian, and that's purely because I was at the BBC working on a different show, which I'd got in[to] by chance, and the lift doors opened one day and Lee Mack walked through those doors and said, 'I've got a comedy show, where are

	the writers?' And I didn't know him at all! I just went, 'Yeah, I'll do it!'
OLIVIA	He said that out loud?
PAUL	He said it out loud as a joke, and I said, 'I'll do it,' and my writing partner at the time was in the toilet, so he didn't get the job, and I did. [*Olivia and Amy laugh.*] So, the lesson surely there is, hold it in!
OLIVIA	Oh my goodness!
PAUL	So, it's those moments and I think it . . . was it Tacitus? I think some Greek scholar who said that opportunity's where preparation and luck meet.
OLIVIA	Yes.
PAUL	And it might have been a comic book, I can't remember. But you know . . . I sort of adhere to that. But I think of course that does miss the other element, which is God. God's plan on us as well.
OLIVIA	Yes.
PAUL	And he has a plan for us. And sometimes we've got to lean on to that and just trust that, because ultimately we don't have that control. God does.
OLIVIA	So, when you think about the timing of that, the fact that Lee Mack's walking out, you're seeing him at that time and how God's planned that. That's just amazing, isn't it?
PAUL	It is, but you could also, you could drive yourself potty thinking, what other opportunities am I . . .
OLIVIA	Have I missed? [*Laughs.*]
PAUL	. . . missing out on, because I've gone there at the wrong moment or that sort of thing? So, you never know. But you have to trust that actually . . . that God's got a greater plan for us.
OLIVIA	Absolutely.
PAUL	. . . We might think we've missed those opportunities, but we haven't. The right opportunity's up ahead.
OLIVIA	Thank you. Amy, I going to ask you something because I think the story of Mary and Martha to me has been something that's really resonated in my life. In fact, I started a charity called Martha's Oasis for a reason . . .
AMY	Oh right!

OLIVIA	. . . because of the thing about Martha. Now you've written quite a lot about Mary and Martha, and about Mary's choices of sitting at the feet of Jesus. Do you want to tell us a little bit more about that and why you've written so extensively about Mary and Martha?
AMY	Yes.
OLIVIA	And the lessons that you've learned from . . .
AMY	Definitely . . .
OLIVIA	. . . from their story?
AMY	Definitely and I don't want to leave out Lazarus either.
OLIVIA	No, oh, Lazarus.
AMY	He can be the forgotten one. He doesn't ever speak in the gospel stories. But . . . and as we were talking about finding our gifts and purpose and who we are in God, Mary did that. She sat at the feet of Jesus . . .
OLIVIA	Yes.
AMY	. . . when culturally that was completely inappropriate. That was just not acceptable for a woman to be sitting basically at the feet of a rabbi, a teacher. But she eschewed cultural convention, and Jesus affirmed her. And who knows what she learned at that time? Now she was the one who anointed his feet, with nard, anointed him for his death. So did she learn from Jesus at that time that he was going to die? We don't know what she learned, but she came into great wisdom as she sat at the feet of Jesus. So, in my book, *Transforming Love*, I look at the three gospel stories. And they're just so amazing, how friendship with Jesus changes us, because God knows us fully and we've got a day-to-day life with Jesus and we keep learning, sitting at his feet, and then we'll find out what are our gifts. Well, sit at the feet of Jesus and you'll maybe be empowered to say, 'I'm here!' [*Olivia laughs.*] 'Choose me! I'll do it!' when the elevator doors open. Sorry, the lift doors. [*Olivia laughs.*]
PAUL	We'll take that, we know what you mean. Don't worry about it, that's fine.
OLIVIA	So, when are you conscious of using your spiritual gifts? And that question can be to either one of you. Gifts are some things that people have made . . . such

a mysterious thing, haven't they? They've made it so mystical. But you both talk about your gifts; you've talked about where God has led you and even how God has provided fortuitous moments for both of you. So, when are you conscious, or most conscious, of when you're using your gifts, your spiritual gifts?

AMY   I think I'm not really conscious of using them and I think that's the beauty of it, is that . . .

OLIVIA   You slide into it.

AMY   . . . I think God is the one who brings it out in us, and oftentimes other people will say, 'Oh, you're so good at this,' or, 'Oh, you really did that well,' and you're like, 'Really? That's me?' And they go, 'That can't be me. So it must be God in me.' I mean, it is you, but . . .

OLIVIA   Yeah.

AMY   . . . I think if we're too aware of it, then it's that whole ego thing. What do you think, Paul?

PAUL   I agree totally . . . I find it really difficult to work out what my gifts are until someone says, 'That really connected with me,' and, as a writer, often it's that solitary thing and, whatever our jobs are out there, it might be that we think, *I'm just working in this kind of private space.* But actually, it's when you get those little honest moments of someone saying, 'You know what? That thing that you said a month ago, a year ago, ten years ago, that really . . . you've set me on a journey here.' So, if we give ourselves more opportunities to encourage other people, we often won't know those results. But . . .

AMY   And you won't remember that.

PAUL   You won't remember it. Totally.

AMY   'Really, did I say that?'

PAUL   Yeah. But it might be decades' time, or you'll never know. But someone says, 'That thing you said, you encouraged me to do that thing and go for that job, or make that change. And it's had an impact and had an effect.' So I think that sense of encouragement and generosity of spirit that we can bring . . . But we don't know it ourselves often. I sort of, I feel like sometimes I'm . . . We went bowling the other day, and my kids had the bumpers up on the side, and I feel like I'm that bowling ball just bouncing back and forth between these bumpers, and I'm not even looking to see if I got a strike or not, but someone else will tell you, years later, 'By the way, that really hit, that really, you know, you got that strike.' Because otherwise I just feel like I'm blindly going back and forth. I don't know what I'm doing, but . . .

AMY   That's an amazing image.

OLIVIA   Yeah.

AMY   So, is God throwing the ball?

PAUL   Yes! I think so. I'm just a bowling ball, that's still, at the last minute sometimes you miss completely and you think, *Ah, I'd get at least one pin over!* We try for the best.

OLIVIA   Thank you. I think we've got time for one more question, so I'm going to ask this one. Have you ever confidently set out on a path, only to discover you were being prompted to turn back, or to change course?

PAUL   Quite probably, yes. I think the difficulty is that as a freelance self-employed jester, essentially [*Olivia laughs*], that so many of my career decisions in my life are unusual and odd, and . . . I set out doing stand-up comedy for years on the mainstream comedy circuit. I still do a little bit there, but for years that meant sort of playing by someone else's rules and trying to fit the rooms that I was in. And after a while, I realised that actually I need to do what I think God wants me to do, and not necessarily play by the rules that society was sort of setting, you know, the temperature of the room at the time, which is to be a bit wild and bawdy and that sort of thing. And in time I've realised that actually, no, that the comedians I really admire, the Milton Jones and Tim Vine and people who, you know, great Christians, [are] comedians who lift the level, raise the bar of the room and still make us all feel that sense of joy . . . And they do it by their rules, not by society's rules, and I think that's really, really good because they're listening to what God wants.

OLIVIA   Such an important thing as a Christian. And what about you, Amy? Have you ever done that? Set out somewhere, thinking, *This is the way to go,* and then had to . . . or been prompted to turn back or to change course?

AMY   Yes, mine is work-related as well. I'm realising that it's not always work-related. This one was when I was trying to shop around that first book that I wrote. And I had been an editor, so I had lots of contacts. I had a hot US agent and blah, blah, blah. And we shopped it around to fifteen different publishers, and all but one said no. And the one that said yes was the one that I was working for at the time, and they didn't want that book.

OLIVIA   Oh, so you had so start again?

AMY   So, I had done all this work and that was very much God protecting me from having that horrible first book out there. And then I wrote what ended up being my first book, which might now be turning into a movie, who knows? [*Olivia gasps.*] But, yeah. So that was very humbling at the time to get all of those no, no, no, no, nos. And to feel so crushed 'cause I had moved into writing as an act of faith, as an act of putting myself out there, and then rejection, rejection, rejection. But I learned my identity is not in being a writer; it's in being God's beloved. So, I think . . . we all have different ways of setting out, trying, and these are big examples, aren't they, but there are small ones in everyday life too of, *Should I turn off the motorway here? Or, Should I go see this person? Should I . . .?* In our everyday life, I think God is leading us and guiding us and helping us as we partner with him . . . to move forward in wonderful life-giving ways. I love your raising-us-up aspect, that's amazing.

OLIVIA   And that's part of the adventure of being with Christ, isn't it, and trying to discover where *your* place is in the world. What is God asking us to do? And often it means going down a blind end, it sometimes seems, and turning around and coming back.

AMY   But Jesus is with you . . .

OLIVIA   Absolutely.

AMY   . . . on that road. You're not . . .

OLIVIA   All the way.

AMY   You're not alone.

OLIVIA   All the way along. You are not alone. Thank you very much for that, Amy. That brings our session to a close. See you at Session 3.

SESSION 3
BEING WITH JESUS AND BECOMING FRUITFUL

OLIVIA	Hello, and welcome to Session 3: Being fruitful and becoming like Jesus. So Amy, Paul, I'm going to ask you a question about life. Now, life is messy much of the time, isn't it? How do you cope with that? How do you both cope with that? And how do you keep your eyes on Jesus throughout all of it?
PAUL	It's tricky, isn't it? It's not easy, and we navigate our way through life. I've got two children; they occupy a lot . . . I'm in the 'dad taxi' phase of life right now, you know, ferrying them across town for different activities and their social calendar's busy and trying to fit . . . We've got the big 'whiteboard of plenty'. On a busy week [*Olivia laughs*] it's full of ink to say who needs to be where and when. And in amongst that, it's difficult. We haven't got a column for Jesus in that. We've got a column for mum and dad and my two kids, and it's where do we find time in it? And I find, in a crisis, I do remember to connect with Jesus and with God. And you know, in the pandemic, we had a really, you know, my work went straight away. My wife was very ill early on with Covid, and it really affected us very quickly. Whereas I've known friends of ours and family who were saying they hadn't really noticed much difference for several months, even. We're going, 'But our world has just turned upside down, for a variety of reasons.' In those times, I really leaned on God very, very quickly. But I think the time that I notice that I drift and I forget to connect with God is when I'm busy, when that whiteboard . . .
OLIVIA	Yes.
PAUL	. . . gets full. And those are times that I need to remember and focus in and go, and this is the time I need to lean on God and say, 'Help me. Get me through this.'
OLIVIA	I love that, 'the whiteboard of plenty'.

PAUL	Hmm. [*Laughs.*]
AMY	It's a good way of looking at it.
OLIVIA	It's a great way of putting it.
AMY	The whiteboard of plenty.
PAUL	Sounds very mystical, doesn't it? Yes. The ring of destiny.
AMY	Not very . . .
PAUL	Very Tolkien.
AMY	Not very mystical.
PAUL	The whiteboard of plenty!
AMY	I love that. Well, life is muddled, and I think . . . I love to be busy, and I think sometimes I get too committed, then it's more, 'Ooh! Eek! Lord, please help me; I can't do this!' Or it's just, you know, following God and pushing ourselves to go outside of our comfort zone and doing the next thing, following those nudges of grace, following those little hints that you hear in the Bible as you read the Bible, or a Christian friend when you're talking to them. How are you hearing God? How are you sensing God leading you? And it's not like he's like this taskmaster making you do these things. It's the partnership, the friendship, the walking hand in hand . . .
OLIVIA	Yeah.
AMY	. . . because of how you're made and your passions. And it's not like God is this taskmaster, like I said, making you do things. He wants you to have a whiteboard of plenty, where you've got good things to do, good things to serve, and it is muddly? And I think we can lose our way when we're not rooting ourselves in spiritual practices. Ways to remember that we're created in God's image and that we love him. So, every time you put the kettle on, practise the presence of Jesus. Every time you go to the loo or wash your hands, remember that you're made in God's image. Building in these practices in the day . . . go for a walk, exercise wonder: 'Lord, you are the creator of the heavens and the earth!' That roots us, and that really helps us when we're crying out to God and going, 'Lord, I don't understand this.

Why has this happened?' Sorry, I'm probably going on too long.

OLIVIA No, no not at all! No, I was just . . .

AMY I'd love to hear what you do too, Olivia.

OLIVIA No, because I was just thinking about . . . We talk about life being messy. And during the pandemic, you will probably know that many people of colour, especially, were disproportionately affected by Covid. And my father passed away during that time of Covid, and I knew lots and lots of friends that *seemed* to be, most of my friends being like me who are people of colour as well, who died during that time. I cannot think of a messier time in my life when I, you know, was crying out about, 'God, what, why is this happening? How does this happen? How do I find you in the mess of all of this?' And so, it's relatively easy for us to have that, you know, the whiteboard of plenty, but when God sometimes just wipes off that whiteboard, there's nothing left on it, and the only words that you write on there are, 'Why?' That's, that's really tough, and that was really tough for me.

But you know, the great thing about that was finding God in the depths of that, and sometimes suffering, difficulties, having to make those difficult choices, are where we find God sometimes, in the messiness of that, and asking why, but not only just asking, but actually putting yourself in the place where you can find the answer. That's also difficult as well, isn't it? But so, so refreshing. I think my journey with Christ changed at that point through loss, as well. And now I'm just, you just become more busy than ever. I'm sure that your lives are similarly as busy, aren't they? With lots of things happening. How do you centre yourselves and keep centred in the busyness of life? So there's messiness and then there's busyness. How do you centre yourselves in that?

PAUL I find it an interesting . . .

OLIVIA Paul?

PAUL . . . an interesting way of looking at it, the way you talk about how it was . . . in the time of the pandemic, it was so empty. You hear often about how God wipes the slate clean.

OLIVIA   Yes.

PAUL   What about when God wipes the whiteboard clean . . .

OLIVIA   Yeah, yeah.

PAUL   . . . and our diary's suddenly empty and he's upended all the things that we rely on, and things that we hold dear, in a mortal way? So, the blankness of that diary was a tricky time. And then the busyness, the repetitive busyness, the way . . .

OLIVIA   Yes.

PAUL   . . . 'Cause, you know, because we can all have busy weeks, but there's also those senses of time where the weeks get repetitively busy. You suddenly go, *I've overfilled my regular commitments*, you know. So, there's those moments where it's not just a busy season or a busy week or two, but it's actually we've taken on a lot, you know. My kids are doing this club and that club and that club, and I'm . . .

OLIVIA   Yeah.

PAUL   I've got that regular commitment and that regular commitment; I've taken too much work on.

OLIVIA   Yeah, why have we taken so much on?

PAUL   Yeah, and there are those times where you think, where in the week is God?

OLIVIA   Yes. Yeah.

PAUL   Where am I allowing time for God to come in? And we can, as you said, we can still be . . . you know, God likes us, I think, to do things. Certainly, we're not necessarily all called to just wipe it completely clear and . . . because in connection with each other, with those relationships, God is there as well . . . But it's, I think, remembering to have that presence of God with you there in the passenger seat with you, or there in the coffee shop with a friend, or in your workplace, whatever it might be. It's just remembering that that is that presence in our lives, I think.

OLIVIA   Yeah, that's so true. And Amy, when have you been particularly conscious of Jesus' presence with you?

AMY   Well, I think it feeds back to what we were saying of the depths of despair, when we naturally reflexively turn to God, *Where are you?* Like Mary and Martha . . . what they both said after Lazarus has died: 'Lord, if you'd been here, my brother wouldn't have died,' and those are the only words we hear from Mary. 'If you'd been here, Lord, my brother wouldn't have died!' And I think in the depths of the questioning and the disappointment and the betrayal and these times, it's easier to turn to God. So, I've definitely felt very close to God in the questioning times. And I've also felt close to God just in the day-to-day. Oh my goodness, I met you on the street! Isn't that fabulous? And I haven't seen you for a while, and you told me about this. And it was this amazing kind of, *Wow, Lord, that's amazing.* Hearing the stories and experiencing the stories of grace when God comes in and *surprises* us! I love that. I love to share and to go, 'Let's notice that. Let's notice that. God was really at work in you. You were really on fire!'

OLIVIA   Yeah. Yeah.

AMY   And to *celebrate* that. And whether we're in paid employment, whether we're volunteering, we're working in the community, we're just being, um, to really know that God partners with us in the hard times, he's there in the hard times, he'll cry at the grave of Lazarus . . .

OLIVIA   Yes.

AMY   . . . and he'll raise Lazarus up again. Or like with Martha, he'll have a discussion, where she says, 'You're the Messiah!' So God is there in all of these times of our lives.

OLIVIA   And how do you *find* the time or do you *make* . . .

AMY   You have to make the time, don't you?

OLIVIA   . . . the time? Because so often we say, 'Well, I'll have to find the time,' and it's usually at the very last bit of the day when sometimes we're so exhausted, we've all got busy diaries, we've all got things that we've got to do, stuff that we've got to do, especially if you're a working mum as well. But how do you actually *make* the time . . .

AMY	You have to . . .
OLIVIA	. . . rather than just *finding* the time?
AMY	You just have to build it in.
OLIVIA	How do you practise God's presence?
PAUL	Well, I think a couple of things that Amy was alluding to, that firstly having that sense of a *pattern* and working out, do I have my Bible study time? Do I go on a dog walk and have that regular time of prayer every day at a certain time? And building those patterns in or a certain time of the week – I'm going to go to that meeting at church, that prayer meeting, whatever it might be. But also, having enough gaps in the diary, enough opportunities that we can go, *D'you know what? I'm gonna have that ability to respond in the moment.* And to be walking past that church and just popping into a random church I don't know, or seeing a friend, a friend calls, 'Let's have a coffee,' you think, *Oh, [that] doesn't fit with my pattern of this week,* but go, 'Yeah, OK. Let's connect . . . looking for those moments . . .
OLIVIA	It's saying yes more often, do you think?
PAUL	. . . that spark us out. Yeah, I just think you can lean on God and find that time in terms of the regular patterns, but also in terms of having enough gaps and the chance to say yes. The chance to actually go, *Yeah, that's not my usual pattern, but actually that might be a place where God wants me to go and find that new turning point in my life or in someone else's.*
AMY	Because you're building the margin into your diary. And I've really had to do that. I'm a retreat leader who wasn't retreating. [*Olivia laughs.*] So, I was very convicted by that. I want to be a retreat leader who retreats.
OLIVIA	Yes.
AMY	But you have to build it, that margin, those gaps, into your diary so you can say yes to the friend.
PAUL	Totally. Someone says, 'Let's go for that coffee,' and you know, I can't fit it in, whatever . . .
AMY	You've got too many things to do.
PAUL	Yeah.

AMY   Too important.

PAUL   Yeah. 'I can give you fifteen minutes.' But actually, what happens if you give them about an hour? You know what happens if you actually listen more?

AMY   You give them. I love that. No! No! I do that too! I do that!

OLIVIA   It's about making the time, isn't it, to do those things that are really important.

PAUL   And as we said back in Session 1: The generosity of time. You know, time is our greatest currency, and if we can give that . . . It's not our time to give, but, you know, if we can spare that for other people, it can be vital.

OLIVIA   Thank you so much. And that brings our session to a close. Thank you.

SESSION 4
WHEN THINGS GO WRONG, AND WAYS OF STAYING ON TRACK

OLIVIA Hello, welcome to Session 4. Session 4 is about When things go wrong and ways of staying on track. And Amy, I'm just gonna jump straight in there with a question to you, because this is how I feel sometimes, about comparing myself with other people. And always feeling that actually, I am the worst one of the two that I've compared myself with. Do you find yourself comparing yourself with others? And how do you cope with that?

AMY Well, I think the thing about comparing ourselves with others is that, OK, so I'm a published author and Paul is a published author. Now, I would maybe not compare myself with Paul because I don't write children's books and I'm not a comedian, as you can tell. But, a devotional writer writing on prayer who sells 500,000 copies, *that* is where I would maybe more easily compare myself because I'm like, *Oh! I'm found wanting*. So . . .

OLIVIA Yeah.

AMY It's . . . I think the comparisons get really more intimate and tough when we're comparing somebody that we're really doing similar things in work or in life. And how do we stay rooted? It just goes back to, 'Lord, what are you calling me to do? And what is your outcome here? If I'm gonna sow this seed, where is it gonna land? And how are you gonna bring it to fruition? And if that seed is only feeding one person, and not 500,000 . . .'

OLIVIA Yeah.

AMY '. . . can I not be happy with that? Because *you're* the gardener. *You're* the one who sends the sun. *You* keep away the weeds. In *your* economy, in *your* world, if *you* think it's enough that one person receives from my blood, sweat and tears . . . then that's good enough.' So it's reminding, reminding, reminding myself that God is the one who has put this, I don't know . . . Paul, do you find that with . . .

OLIVIA   Yeah, can I ask you that, Paul?

AMY   . . . the comparison kind of thing?

PAUL   Yeah, absolutely. I think it is something . . . to be honest, I've struggled with it. I've struggled with it a lot as a comedian. And I know a lot of comedians do that. I know comedians at the top of their game who are looking over their shoulder going, *But how do I stay here? Am I the best at this? When's my moment gonna go?* And it's so easy to, in any business, I think, to look at others as rivals. And weirdly, a few years ago, I sort of turned it around and thought, *Actually, the people who I thought of as my rivals and my competitors, I'm gonna turn it around completely and I'm gonna make sure that I'm going above and beyond to try and be nice to them and helpful and encouraging.* And I feel so much better about it. It was like a weight lifted. And it helps them. They're surprised, going, 'I thought we were in competition, but you're helping me?' And it turns it on its head. And I've found that sort of connectedness has helped deal with my own jealousies and insecurities a lot better.

OLIVIA   Glad you used that 'J' word actually about jealousy because comparison is so difficult at times, isn't it? Especially when you think someone comes across much better than you do. Someone says something much better. Oh, I wish I'd written that book and I wish I'd written it in exactly that way. And then the feeling of insecurity finds its way into jealousy and makes you think, *If only I was as good as that person.* How would you protect yourself against, or would you recognise jealousy as part of that insecurity or that comparison part of being a Christian? How do you protect yourself against that, do you think?

PAUL   I think you need to constantly be in check about it . . .

OLIVIA   Yeah.

PAUL   . . . and be aware of it.

OLIVIA   Yeah.

PAUL   And I think we can all . . . jealousy and envy and all that, they're all human qualities that we end up with and we can resort to. But it's in the Ten Commandments about not coveting what your neighbour's got, basically. It's there on a tablet etched into stone [*Olivia laughs*], thousands of years ago. And it's something we can all feel. And also, the thing with jealousy is, it feels so natural and yet . . .

OLIVIA   Yes.

PAUL   . . . we'll never be happy.

OLIVIA   Yes.

PAUL   We will never be happy if we're constantly looking at, *How do I get what that person's got over there?* And it just doesn't work. Instead, all you can do is look, be the best that you can be, who God calls us to be. And the great thing about Christianity is God's saying to us, 'You are enough.'

You know, I saw the *Barbie* film recently. [*Paul makes reference to a well-known line from the film.*] It's enough to just be you and be the best you can be, and who God has called you to be. Rather than try and be that person over there. They're that person and they've got their own insecurities and their own things going on. But you are this person. Be the best one you can be, who God calls you to be.

OLIVIA   And yet that sounds so great, doesn't it, Amy, that we say that we are enough and we know it in our heads? But how do you recognise that you are enough before God? How does that work itself out for you, practically?

AMY   Well, in my own personal walk with God, with, you know, reading the Bible and praying and sensing his presence, but also with my mates, with my husband, my family. You know, we need others to help us to follow on what you were saying, Paul. We need others to go, 'OK, don't be jealous,' or, 'Look at what *you're* doing! Let's take a moment and celebrate.'

You know, it's a spiritual discipline to celebrate. And I think we don't do that enough, because it's a way of giving thanks. And expressing gratitude. And I think as we practise gratitude, we also go, 'Wow, I don't have to be jealous, 'cause look at . . . this happened and that happened and this amazing thing happened. And if I'm so worried about what they're doing or what I'm missing out on, what's not happening to me, then you start not being grateful for the amazing things.

And, you know, and we have our friends that we can just . . .

OLIVIA   Right.

AMY   . . . cry with, and say, 'OK, I can't tell anybody else but you, but oh my word! I feel so jealous because so and so had this happen.' And they'll be like, 'OK, well, get it out, rant away. But then, remember when this happened to you? Remember when that happened? Let's take a moment and celebrate.' What do you do, Olivia?

OLIVIA   I think I depend on friends to be able to tell me when things are great and when things are not so great. And also to call out the bad stuff, too. And that's where you need good friends, you know, whether . . . you see them every day or not. I think I find that having good friends who will celebrate with me, the good things that I do that are great, but also say, 'Well, Olivia, I'm not quite sure you're doing that right. Perhaps we can look at it another way.' What you don't need is someone who's absolutely condemning you, because the Bible tells us that you're not condemned, right? So we know about that, but just having someone who'll just keep it real. I love that phrase, 'keeping it real'.

And Paul, I'm going to turn to you and ask you about insecurities. How do you live and manage insecurity and uncertainty?

PAUL   Well, again, it's a . . .

OLIVIA   Probably touched a bit on it already.

PAUL   Yeah, I think so. And it's a core part of life. And it's something, it's not easy. None of this stuff that we're saying is easy. You know, well I . . . I don't want anyone to think that I'm here, I've got it all worked out because this is how I live my life. This is what I'm aiming towards in my life, you know. Life is unstable, you know, and we have stability in God, but . . . when

I was a child, I had a lot of medical issues. I was in Great Ormond Street Hospital for a significant chunk of my childhood. And, you know, months at a time, missed a lot of school and all those things. And I think, for me, it meant that I was asking those fairly big questions really early on from the age of sort of 5, 6, 7. I was in there. You know, my parents would visit, but we were in Cornwall for a lot of this. And I was up in London in the hospital. So they'd come and visit, and stay when possible. But, a lot of time to just puzzle out those big questions of life and mortality and spirituality, and a sense of puzzling out the world, you know. And oddly, a very rare condition I've got, my basically, if I can, you know, I had some internal organs that were on the outside, which isn't ideal. And they're, they're back in now, I'm pleased to say! [*Olivia laughs.*] But they had a lot of operations to solve at the time. And in this quite rare condition I've got, they did a study and a third of people with this went into healthcare as a career. And a third went into entertainment, which is a [*Olivia laughs*] *huge* amount of people.

AMY   Wow!

PAUL   But basically you're in hospital as a kid, and you think, *I want to either heal people or cheer them up,* you know. And that's certainly what I did. You know, there are other comedians and clowns and jesters and comedy writers and authors who've had a lot of time in hospital as a kid. Because you puzzle out those things and think, *What do I want to do with my life? Do I want to connect with people in a way that hopefully elevates and lifts them where they are?* And I think a lot of people do.

OLIVIA   Did you consciously have that then, when you were in hospital thinking about, *What do I want to do?* And . . . you said something about cheering them up or healing them. Did you actually *think* those thoughts?

PAUL   I think so! I didn't think it was a career choice at the time. But I certainly went through my childhood doing that, you know, and trying to be, not the joker as such, but just trying to cheer things along and trying to write comedy and just tell jokes and things like that.

You know, you asked the question about the instabilities of these things. And I think I learned early on that life is unstable and the things we can rely on, you know, for *all of us*, when our walks of life, at some point in life, you hit those sort of medical moments or those crisis moments – it can be delayed by decades, but it happens at some point or other – and therefore, how do we cope with those when they arrive? You know, I had mine quite early, in a way, or one of them. And it was a stumbling block that made me realise that actually, yes, things are unstable, if you rely on mortal things. And therefore, we can look to God and God can help us through that. And I'll walk with Christ, you know.

OLIVIA   Amen. What about you, Amy, about living with uncertainty and insecurity? Has that surfaced in your life or . . . ?

AMY   Actually, growing up, *I* was the one who was the child at home and my brother was the one in hospital. He had lots and lots of health difficulties, and . . . that was really interesting because it affects the whole family, as I'm sure it did with your family. And I was the middle child, so there's all that, too. But we were a Christian family and we relied on God. And we learned how to just, you know, what would be the next thing coming and how do you trust in God in that? So that was really a foundational thing growing up.

And then there have been other periods. When I was 19, one of my best friends was killed in a car accident. So that was a huge moment of those big things like you were doing in hospital of, 'OK, Lord, who are you? Why does this happen? Why did you allow this?' All those big things. 'Am I going to turn from you? Am I going to cling to you?' I did the clinging thing.

OLIVIA   Yeah.

AMY   But trying to figure out these big things in life, and moving away from Minnesota where I grew up, moving east, going to Washington, DC, and then coming over the great big pond. And, you know, it was only supposed to be five to seven years, and here we are, twenty-five years, marrying my English husband, and . . . So lots of uncertainties and instability. *Am I ever going to live in the same country as my parents again? Am I ever going to enjoy good plumbing?* Yes, I do! [*Olivia and Paul laugh.*]

OLIVIA   What do you mean? Excellent plumbers!

AMY   I don't know. Living in vicarages, we do have good plumbing.

OLIVIA   All right, yeah.

AMY   We do have good plumbing, but . . . So how do we rely on God? How do I actually rely on God? How do I put into practice what I am writing about? That's very challenging to me. Am I going to trust God when I don't know what the next gig is? Or not that I do gigs, but, you know, the next job or the next thing. If I'm worried about my kids or my husband or my friends or all these things, am I actually going to believe what I write and what I speak?

OLIVIA   Thank you so much for sharing that. I mean, Amy, let me just ask you another question about *partnering* with God, because you talked about *walking* with him. And when we're talking about *partnering* with God, how do you make that a reality in your life? You know, we love to quote Scripture about, well, 'God's always with me, you know, I'm with him, he's with me.' But when you are *partnering* with him, how does that play out in your daily actions and activities?

AMY   Definitely. Well, you write about in your course so wonderfully, you write about life with Christ and how we abide in Jesus. And it's this mystery that, I mean, I will not go off, but I could talk all day about Christ living in us, and how Christ indwells in us through the Holy Spirit. And we partner with him. And it's such an amazing mystery. And it *is* a mystery. But it's, you know, even in our off times, we've been talking about these nudges of grace . . .

OLIVIA   Yes.

AMY   . . . where we're hearing God and we're sensing God because we're open. We're noticing where God is speaking to us.

I just got a text from a friend who had a dream, a very important dream. God can speak to us in dreams.

OLIVIA   Yes.

AMY   It's about being open and noticing and reading the Bible, and praying and saying, 'Lord, what does this passage mean to me?' So, and then partnering is really just moving forward. 'So, what's my passion? How am I going to pursue that? Lord, can you open the door?'

OLIVIA   Yeah.

AMY   'Will you close the door? Is this door being closed? Is this door open? Should I walk through it? Yeah, let's go through this one. Oh, wow, that side window came open! Should I walk through that or should I climb through that? Or are you closing this one and why?' So, yeah, I mean, how do you partner day by day? I would love to hear.

OLIVIA   Yeah. So partnering for me is that sense of abiding, isn't it? And I'm always fascinated by the fact that God partners with us.

AMY   Yeah, yes.

OLIVIA   When you think about the almighty God partners with us and that he actually doesn't do anything without me – and he could do! But he still loves me enough to put me in as part of that action. I just think that's amazing. And he will hold his response for me. You know, he will wait for me to pick up on something and wants me to share the joy of that. I mean, how do you feel about that, Paul?

PAUL   Yeah.

OLIVIA   Does that resonate with you?

PAUL   . . . Totally. Well, I think what's brilliant for me about the Christian faith is the great mystery of it, that it's the one where Jesus is a person in history. You know, regardless whether you're Christian or not, Jesus exists in the history books. He's there.

OLIVIA   Yes.

PAUL	God has walked the walk and talked the talk as man, as us.
OLIVIA	Yes. He knows what it feels like.
PAUL	Totally, exactly.
OLIVIA	He knows!
PAUL	So that sense that we can talk, rather mystically, quite right, too, about that God is in our lives and how does that work? And it's the great mystery that we can never quite comprehend. But to know that God has done that because he has been here and Jesus has suffered. He's walked the life . . .
OLIVIA	Yes.
PAUL	. . . the human life. He's suffered. He's had that connectedness with humans, with fellow walkers on that journey.
OLIVIA	The loss and pain.
PAUL	Yeah, totally. And those wonderful moments you read in the gospel of those connections of Jesus walking with people, hearing their stories and making a difference in their lives. I think that's when we're partnering with God, there's a sense of that as well.
OLIVIA	Absolutely. That's such a blessing. Thank you both so much for contributing to that. Thank you. That's the end of this session.

SESSION 5
IT'S ALL GOOD – HOW GOD CHANGES EVERYTHING

OLIVIA   Hello, welcome to Session 5: It's all good – how God changes everything. And Paul, I'm going to start with you. Can you think of a time when you were burned out, or someone you know was burned out and found themselves unexpectedly blessed?

PAUL   Yes, I can think of that. Certainly. The one that really strikes me is in the pandemic, once again, when we had, not just Covid in our house, but then long Covid, which stuck around for, for quite a while. And a certain family member was unable really to do much then beyond going downstairs and then beyond the garden. And, of course, this was a very bleak time for many, many reasons. But it was then once those daily walks could increase a little bit, we bumped into her, someone we didn't really know, turns out to be a neighbour of ours, who was just a complete blessing, because she was there doing some gardening in the field behind our house, which belongs to the church, it turns out. And it's not a church we'd been to. It's our nearest church. We were driving across town to this other church . . .

OLIVIA   And there's a church behind you.

PAUL   . . . and we've discovered this church – not discovered, it was there all along! But, by meeting the people, meeting that particular person, in fact, was a total blessing on our family because it was the connection that we needed to help us back into the outside world again, and help us from a place of ill health into a place of not just physical health but spiritual health as well. And we, we found a real family in that church. And that's really down to that one person who was in the right place at the right time, doing some gardening, in what felt like . . . You know, the Bible begins with a garden . . .

OLIVIA   It does!

PAUL   . . . and, you know, God tends the creation and plants us here to be part of that, which is wonderful.

AMY   And it ends with a garden, too.

OLIVIA   Yeah. I was thinking exactly the same thing! What about you, Amy?

AMY   Well, I think of a story that my husband has given me permission to share because it was when he was really burnt out and having a hard time, a lot of stuff going on with his family of origin, with work, all these kinds of things. And he didn't sense God and he couldn't pray. And all he could do was read the Psalms, the ancient prayerbook in the Bible, other people's prayers. And when he had no prayers at all, that's what he did every day. 'Cause he's got this really good, 'I'm going to keep on keeping on.' And he did . . . even when it was bleak. There appeared to be no God. I mean, he knew intellectually that there was, just praying . . . the prayers of other people. And that's how God can meet us in these really bleak times, through his word, through unexpected meetings that we have with gardens, and . . . God has a way of breaking through, doesn't he? How about you, Olivia?

OLIVIA   Good question. I think I've written about it as part of the York Course, but I remember several months ago now just being so tired, just so exhausted. Grief can be exhausting, right? It's grief and all the things about motherhood sometimes, as a single mum, and just feeling that I was just not going to make this, and being completely at my wits' end . . . *What do I do?* I was trying every single retreat I possibly could find. No spaces. And then, someone said, 'Well, why don't you try this particular person and this particular retreat? And it's all free.' *Free? Free!* And it was. And at that state where I just thought, *I just cannot cope any more,* someone had opened their house and allowed me to just go and to sit and to just be, which was just amazing. So that was such a blessing to me. One, because it was free. That's amazing. But also, where it was, you know, right by the coast, watching the seascape, it was just an amazing thing, and was really recuperative to me, especially dealing with things that sometimes you just don't know you got all that stuff . . . that's been surfacing and . . . or stuff that you've repressed, and then it comes back up again.

So that was just such a great time of being able to, to be blessed by others, but also recognising burnout. And I think one of the things we've got to recognise as Christians – it doesn't really matter where you are and what job you do – how you recognise burnout. Would you be able to give a little inkling or insight about how you recognised that you are getting burned out, that you are stressed, that you are super busy? How would you recognise that in your own lives?

PAUL   And that stress thing is something that we need to be aware of. Absolutely. And it's historically often been seen as a weakness to acknowledge burnout or to be burnt out. But it's a real strength if you know when to stop . . .

OLIVIA   Yes.

PAUL   . . . and when to pause and to acknowledge that in yourself. And know, *I just need a bit of time here. I need a moment. I need a while*, you know, whatever.

OLIVIA   And it's not a weakness.

PAUL   Not a weakness at all. It is an absolute strength to know when to do that. 'Cause it then means that you are better equipped to look after yourself and look after those around you in your family, your friends. That's what God wants us to be – someone who is strong in themselves, in their own lives and aware of when we need to stop to look after ourselves, to then be the best person we can be.

OLIVIA   Absolutely. I think part of what our modern life is that we measure ourselves by saying, 'How are you?' 'I'm OK. You know, I'm fine.' Or, or we measure ourselves by being busy, don't we? 'I'm busy. How busy are you?' We measure each other against each other's busyness [*Paul laughs*], as though that's some sort of accolade. How do you recognise that you're getting burned out, Amy?

AMY   Well, I think talk to those living with me. They'll tell you immediately. Aagh! You know, stop being cranky and stop being short, and . . . because we are limited people, aren't we? We're limited in what we can do. And we shouldn't think that we have to be super busy and we have to always be doing this and doing that.

But . . . so it's learning to embrace rest. And I have one of my dearest friends has very severe ME. And so she's bed-bound. And I have learned from her how to rest better . . .

OLIVIA   To stop.

AMY   And it's for . . . rest is different for everybody. For some person, it might be gardening for fifteen minutes, for another it might be streaming a show, um, for another, going for a walk, for another, a chat with a friend – not for introverts like you and me, Olivia. [*Everyone laughs.*] But, um, the people living with you can often tell you when you're being burnt out because you're not . . . I shouldn't say *you* . . . *I'm* not a nice person to live with when I'm burnt out.

OLIVIA   Neither am I. Neither am I.

PAUL   Well, I should, I should acknowledge and apologise that today, when I've met Amy today here in this wonderful place, I remember distinctly, I said to you, 'So are you well and busy?' And as I said it . . .

OLIVIA   Yeah!

PAUL   . . . I thought, *I'm equating busyness with a good thing* . . .

OLIVIA   With a good thing . . .

PAUL   But actually, you know, you can be good busy, you can be bad busy, you can be all sorts of different types of busy and sometimes well, and not busy and not well, and busy and all of these different things.

AMY   And I didn't even notice; it didn't register with me.

PAUL   I thought as I said it . . .

OLIVIA   We're so used to it, aren't we? Yeah. I think we're so used to it.

PAUL   Just checking how we are, acknowledging other people's busyness.

OLIVIA   Yeah.

PAUL   'Oh good, you're busy. Oh, that's good.' Yeah. I mean, is it? I don't know.

AMY   You're being useful. You're useful.

OLIVIA   Yeah.

AMY   We don't have to be useful, do we?

PAUL   Agree.

OLIVIA   And so we're thinking about, and this session talks about God's presence changing everything. And we've received so much. We've talked about the generosity of God as we went through the earlier sessions. But Paul, because we've received so much from God, and because he's been so good and we've been in his presence, we've talked a little bit about that as well, how do you then share God's abundance and his abundance with others?

PAUL   Well, I think, you know, we are part of a community, a church community, a town, a city, a village, whatever it might be. And we have places within that community. It doesn't, as we're just saying though, it doesn't mean you have to be a busy pillar of the community, and therefore I must be governor of that school. I must set up that cause there. I must go and support that thing and commit to that once a week. But living in community with one another, and working out when we can share our gifts, and when we can share what we have, and make sure that actually, you know, we, we are individually wonderful. We are fearfully and wonderfully made, and we can be beacons where we live, you know, and for those around us and that . . . The person I mentioned earlier – the member of our local church who was just quietly doing some gardening, and yet the impact that she had on our family, and that's just us, on others as well, just by being who she is in our community – is a beacon and is to be commended. And we can all, we are all called in different ways sometimes to . . . God uses us to connect with other people. And we will often never know just what impact we've made.

AMY   And I think that's so important what you're saying about how God has made us.

OLIVIA	Yes.
AMY	And that so strikes me that, because he is delighted when we put our passions into play. So, your friend was gardening. Or somebody else is doing something that they love doing. And that's how God can reach out through them. I have a dear friend who's very, very, very introverted and she found herself very prayerful, a bit mystical, but just like too 'innered', as it were. And so God called her out, and now she is an intercessor for all of these different ministries.

So she's still mainly at home. She's alone, with Jesus, but she's now in touch with all of these people, supporting, giving amazing prayer support for these ministries around the world. So it honours who she is. And I just love that. So, as the people who are taking this course and talking about it, it's like affirming, Olivia, I love that you do this and you're so good at administration and all of this. And Paul, I love that you're doing this and calling forth the best out of them, out of our mates and our, the people that are in our small groups, and maybe the ones that we find difficult. [*Olivia laughs.*]

OLIVIA	Um, especially those.
AMY	Especially those. That's right. Calling forth the best in them because that's how God has created them to be.
PAUL	Well, I know in our church, we've got people who are great encouragers, just on a private one to one. They're not the best public speakers, but they are privately brilliant encouragers, but I know others who are great public speakers. Not so good one on one, but can encourage and enthuse the masses. And I just remembered when you said about the intercessors. We have a guy in our church who does the prayers, the intercessions, and he, he has a way with language and it is poetry, and it makes us feel greater compassion and empathy with others, the way that he speaks about the world and our fellow human beings. And that is a gift in itself. And these people, and often these people need to be told now and then like, 'That thing you do there, that's really good!' Because otherwise they can

OLIVIA AMARTEY is Executive Director for the Elim Pentecostal Church, having previously worked in senior leadership positions in the NHS. She is also Associate Pastor of Crosspoint Church, a church plant based in north Birmingham, and has a passion for sharing God's word creatively. Much appreciated for her sense of fun, Olivia was a lively contributor to David Wilbourne's well-received York Course, *You Can Be Serious!* (2023). She is a member of the board of Essential Christian, the parent charity of Spring Harvest.

PAUL KERENSA is a stand-up comedian and scriptwriter for *Miranda, Not Going Out* and, most recently, *TFI Friday* and *Top Gear*. He appears regularly on BBC Radio 2's *Pause for Thought*, and is the author of several humorous books for children.

AMY BOUCHER PYE is a London-based writer, speaker, retreat leader and spiritual director. She is the author of six books, including *Transforming Love: How friendship with Jesus changes us* and *7 Ways to Pray.*

The C. S. Lewis quote on p. 32 is from *The Collected Letters of C. S. Lewis, vol. 3* by CS Lewis © copyright 1963, 1964 CS Lewis Pte Ltd. Extract used with permission.

OUR WARM THANKS to Monkeynut for recording and producing the course audio and video. Photography © xxx

York Courses: https://spckpublishing.co.uk/bible-studies-and-group-resources/york-courses

	shrink away and not realise this. So, I need to tell that guy he's really good.
AMY	Yeah.
OLIVIA	You can call it out.
AMY	Do that.
OLIVIA	We call it out in people, don't we? And say to people, 'You're good at this. Have a go.' So, what would you say to people who are watching or listening to this course? We've been talking about the gift of God, we've talked about his generosity. We've talked about how God's presence changes everything. How would you encourage them to use their gifts right now?
PAUL	I'm going to say, there's that thing of, if you can, be generous, you know . . .
OLIVIA	Yes.
PAUL	. . . and it doesn't mean about money, and you know, time, as we've said, is hugely valuable. But at the same time, it's not I think that we need to just think that our time and our money or our energy, our resources, ourselves don't matter. It's because they do matter. And our time has a value. You know we . . .
OLIVIA	It does.
PAUL	. . . if I give my time to someone, as I know it's with giving time once again, but if I have time and skills or encouragement, whatever it might be, God has seized that there's value in that . . .
OLIVIA	Yes.
PAUL	. . . because it's God-given. And it's because God values that . . .
OLIVIA	Yeah.
PAUL	. . . that we can value that as well. So when we actually have that time, attention and energy for other people, it's because God puts such value in it . . .
OLIVIA	He does.
PAUL	. . . that when we give it to others, if we can, you know, if they're expecting a ten-minute chat and you can give them an hour; if you can listen and really truly listen . . .
OLIVIA	Yeah.
PAUL	. . . I think those things can be so valuable to people.
OLIVIA	Absolutely brilliant. I mean, I love the, the idea of

walking along with someone and encouraging them to be at the best that they can be. And it's not just a pop psychology, is it, it's much more than that. It's recognising that everyone has a gift, and God asks us to help those who, who probably don't even recognise it sometimes, but just to walk along in that gift. What would you say about that, Amy?

AMY   Well, I would say, 'Have a go,' you know.

OLIVIA   Just try it.

AMY   Yeah, have a go. You might not feel confident. You might feel the impostor syndrome that we've been talking about, but go, 'OK, Lord, are you calling me into this? I'm going to try it.' And again, pushing those doors and windows that we were talking about as well. I think God loves to bless our tiny efforts.

OLIVIA   Yeah.

AMY   Think about the mustard seed turning into a big tree, or you think about the loaves and the fish. These meagre provisions, and Jesus just multiplies them. So he'll do that with our gifts. If we have a willing heart, if we have some elbow grease, then go ahead and have a go. And you could be amazed at how God blesses your teeny efforts because he's God . . .

OLIVIA   Yes.

AMY   . . . and he's created you in his image, and he loves you. And he loves it when you get out there and try to change the world.

OLIVIA   You were saying something earlier about the mustard seed, and you also mentioned an earlier session about being a spiritual director. And I know, I was ministering to some women this weekend gone, and they were saying, 'Oh, I don't have any gifts, God. I've got nothing.' And what they're doing is comparing themselves to the public gift – the thing that they think is just so great because you're out there doing all that. How would you encourage someone to be able to see that what they have is not insignificant to God? How would you encourage them in that?

AMY   Well, it's what we've been talking about, isn't it? Have your mates, you know, ask your friends, 'What do you see in me?'

OLIVIA   Yeah.

AMY   'What do you see as the gifts? What sparks joy in me? How do you see me coming to life?' And God! Ask God: 'Show me! I'm going to set aside ten minutes every day for thirty days . . .'

OLIVIA   Yeah, that's a good way.

AMY   '. . . as just a way of saying, "Lord, I'm serious about this." Not that you won't tell me on Day 2, but just that I want to really say this is important.' And to pray, to ask trusted others and to just search the Bible and then, do what . . .

OLIVIA   I like that.

AMY   . . . you're excited to do!

OLIVIA   I like the fact that you're making time intentionally for that. What would you say, Paul, just to wrap this?

PAUL   Yeah, I think it is that we're talking often about the outward-facing, and where we can connect with other people. And I think it starts though, with ourselves and with finding that worth in ourselves. 'Cause sometimes you said those people you were speaking to go, 'Well, I don't know my gift. Have I got any?' In fact, it's not even saying, 'I don't know what they are.' It's saying, 'I haven't got any!'

OLIVIA   Yeah, 'cause they're saying, 'It's all right for you, Olivia, because you're telling us this. Well, I don't have what you have.' Little do they know . . . the costs! But, yeah . . .

PAUL   Absolutely. And we do all individually have such marvellous gifts. And I've known people, I've seen people who thought they didn't have anything going on. But then you bump into them five years later and they now go, 'Oh . . . I've trained as a teacher and I'm doing this.' And you see them again three years after that, they go, 'And now I'm coaching this, that, the other, and I've got to see these generations grow up and grow through.' They have done such marvellous things, and we can encourage others to find that encouragement within themselves, because if we can find that individual, that worth that we have, that God has instilled in us so many of these marvellous things, and then that's when it can overflow and spread into others, and be positive and be a great beacon into the world.

OLIVIA   Perfect way to wrap up. Thank you so much for that, Paul. Thank you, Amy, for being with me on this journey. Thank you.